ENDOR

There are messages that carry a "for such a time as this" edge to them. Why? Because they demand a response due to the urgency of the hour. In a world where it seems like everything is being turned upside down, and truth is being regularly redefined, *Holy Revolution* is a prophetic wake-up call to every single believer. Holiness was common language among the awakeners of old—those who were catalysts for church revival and societal awakening. It's only in recent decades that we seem to have "trended" away from holiness, not because it's unnecessary or irrelevant, but because our view and definition of "holiness" became confounded with legalism. Holiness is not a spiritual to-do list that keeps God happy with us. The holiness outlined in these pages introduces you to a fresh perspective on how a new breed of rising millennial leaders see things. It all centers on being saturated by God—and this author will stir your heart to desire it! In a period of history where believers are unsettled, this book will provoke you to rise above the noise and venture higher and go farther. It calls you into a place of divine communion with heaven, not simply so you can spend more time in a "prayer closet," but so that when you interact with your sphere of influence, you demonstrate the "difference" of heaven on earth in real ways. This difference gives you the ability to tap into the thoughts of the Holy Spirit and release strategies for the problems no one else can solve. This difference is accessing new creative expressions that reveal the beauty, power, and relevancy of God to a world that is hungry to know Him. This difference is living protected and supernaturally shielded from the tactics of the enemy by discovering a new place of divine security. This book isn't a byproduct of a theorist but rather, an experienced practitioner. I've seen it in action. Jamie Lyn is my daughter-in-law and she lives what she writes. What gives this message substance and power is the fact that she literally walks it out before our eyes. You'll experience a fresh gust of supernatural wind as you walk through these pages with her!

Lance Wallnau
Bestselling Author of *God's Chaos Code*
LanceWallnau.com

Jamie Lyn has been a dear friend to Lorisa and me for many years. I have had a front-row seat to God's divine orchestration of her calling and ministry. She is a voice that needs to be heard in this season. *Holy Revolution* is a trumpet blast for this hour. God is calling a Jacob generation to ascend His hill and stand in His holy place with clean hands and pure hearts. This is a road map for us. Thank you, Jamie Lyn, for modeling these pages in your life over the years.

MICHAEL and LORISA MILLER
Upper Room Global Directors
www.URDallas.com

Jamie Lyn Wallnau's book *Holy Revolution* is a well of wisdom, direction, revelation, and insight for this new era. These pages burn with the purity of His heart, the fire of His love, the weight of His truth, and the call to living a life set apart. This is not a "read once" book. This is one to have in a place of easy access to continue to go back and read through this new era. This marvelous book is a gift from God to the Church, keys for the era, and the fire of the Lord to bring alignment, deeper purification, and a great arising of the burning ones. Jamie Lyn, thank you for this glorious book! It's a game changer!

LANA VAWSER
Lana Vawser Ministries
lanavawser.com

The Holy Revolution was birthed out of an authentic encounter with God. I'll never forget the day that it happened. Jamie Lyn had such a profound encounter with God that she was left undone and had to retreat with her mother into my old office. When she came out of the office, her eyes were swollen like chocolate marshmallows and mascara rivers were caked down her cheeks. It was a sight! But it was holy. She was different, and the fear of the Lord was tangibly present. She had encountered the holiness of God. Unfortunately, *holy* is one of those words that conjures up thoughts of "goodie two shoes," "holier than thou," or even judgmental. But nothing could be further from the truth. True holiness is radical, pure, adventuresome, countercultural, and revolutionary! When you meet someone who has encountered an aspect of the Lord, they have the ability to transmit that understanding to others in a way that normal head knowledge can't do. This book will revolutionize your life. It's time for the revolutionaries to arise, not birthed out of bitterness and dissatisfaction with the current state of affairs, but with a holy love for the world that sets it on fire to be set apart with true value once again!

Michael Mauldin
Founder, I Am Journey
Co-founder, Song Lab
www.iamjourney.co

In today's culture wars, Jamie Lyn's message of a Holy Revolution is more important than ever. In a world full of Christian compromise, Jamie is calling the church back to its mandate of holiness. For anyone wanting to live a set apart life for Christ, this book is a must read.

CATHERINE MULLINS
Catherine Mullins Ministry
catherinemullins.com

A word fitly spoken is like apples of gold in a setting of silver. Practical, insightful, and winsome, Jamie Lyn speaks of the path of holiness in a way that we can all understand. This book will challenge, convict, and inspire you to follow the narrow path and to shine like stars in a crooked and perverse generation! I'm thankful for her life and for this book that I pray will start a Holy Revolution!

Peter K. Louis
Founder of Braveheart Ministries
braveheartministries.org

Holiness is a blessing and a delight! And I am convinced that this book, *Holy Revolution*, is a key catalyst for what the Spirit of God wants to produce in the earth among believers. Jamie Lyn Wallnau presents holiness, not as some legalistic list of dos and don'ts. Hardly. As an artist, she paints a beautiful picture of what a life saturated in the presence of God can look like and the impact it has on the world. Holiness is not about what we have to deny; it's about becoming completely yielded to Jesus *so that* the life of Jesus can flow through us without hindrance. God is raising up an end-time army who advance with love and power into every sphere of society where darkness has been unchallenged and uncontested. I believe *Holy Revolution* is a must-read for every believer who desires to witness this Holy Spirit transformation released in their lives and to their world!

LARRY SPARKS, MDIV
Publisher, Destiny Image
lawrencesparks.com

Dedication

For Timothy, Holly, Lance Carl, Joy, and our future bloodlines. May the generations we birth and raise live this message with hearts fully open to the leadership of Jesus! May we all live the life of abundance knowing He is our everything.

Thank you, Papa, Grandma, Nana, and Grandaddy for who you are and how you have labored for us to be here today. I love you.

HOLY REVOLUTION

FINDING TRUE SATISFACTION
IN A LIFE SET APART

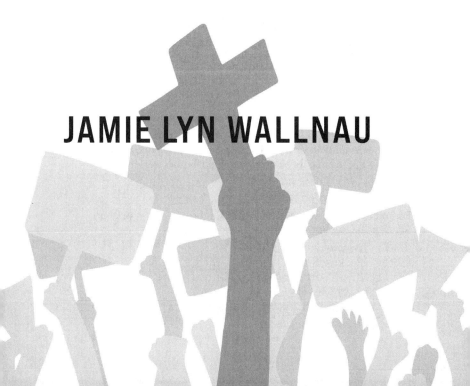

JAMIE LYN WALLNAU

DESTINY IMAGE® PUBLISHERS, INC.

P.O. Box 310, Shippensburg, PA 17257-0310

"Promoting Inspired Lives."

This book and all other Destiny Image and Destiny Image Fiction books are available at Christian bookstores and distributors worldwide.

Cover design by Eileen Rockwell
Interior design by Terry Clifton

For more information on foreign distributors, call 717-532-3040.

Reach us on the Internet: www.destinyimage.com.

ISBN 13 TP: 978-0-7684-5785-8
ISBN 13 eBook: 978-0-7684-5786-5
ISBN 13 HC: 978-0-7684-5788-9
ISBN 13 LP: 978-0-7684-5787-2

For Worldwide Distribution, Printed in the U.S.A.

1 2 3 4 5 6 7 8 / 25 24 23 22 21

ACKNOWLEDGMENTS

Lance Wallnau, Jr.: I love you and am honored to be your wife. You are a champion of heaven. Pure and set apart. Thank you for being you.

Mom and Dad: Thank you for being not just my parents but my spiritual parents as well. You sacrificed much to make room for Timothy, Holly, and me to know Jesus. You raised me to know God and never silenced the crazy things we didn't have language for, yet. I love our family.

Holly and Timothy: I love you both and I am grateful to have siblings like you. You are treasures in my heart. Thank you for always supporting and cheering me on. I believe in you.

Patricia King: You are a hero of faith and I cannot say thank you enough for serving our generation with your love and with an uncompromising example of what this message really looks like. Thank you for believing in me and celebrating everyone so well. You have taught me by the way you live your life in true abundance. Love you.

Sharla: I love you. Thank you for introducing my mom to the Holy Spirit. He has changed our lives forever and knowing you has done the same. I could say so much here. You are family forever.

Michael and Lorisa: Thank you for being patient with me and loving me through my 20s as I grew up in front of you and with you. Your "yes" even when hard times came has changed thousands of lives already, including my own. You are the real deal. His presence really has transformed our lives forever. Much of this book was ignited alongside both of you and our UR family.

Ashley: You're the real MVP. Thank you for reading each chapter as it was finished. If anyone doesn't like it, I'll send them to you, lol.

Mauldin and Meredith: Thank you for championing Lance and me beyond our comfort zones and past our fears. Thank you for stirring creativity in us both and for officiating and being in our wedding and being in our lives. You are changing the world through creative reformation.

Destiny Image: You are all amazing and I am so deeply honored that you would choose to publish this piece of work. Thank you Larry, Tina, Christian, John, Shaun, Tammy, and all for all you do to help get the gospel out there!

To you holding this book: May the Spirit of God remind you of your own precious moments with Him along the way that have prepared you for this holy revolution. We need you. Let's go!

CONTENTS

FOREWORD

Born in Canada in 1951, I was raised by both parents in a conservative, "non-churchgoing" family. Most Canadians in that generation believed they were Christians in that they respected Christian values and, for certain, when asked to fill out a survey, if they were not a Buddhist, Muslim, or Hindu, they would put a confident mark in the box next to Christian (the first option on the list). Canada, the United States, and other western nations at the time were identified as "Christian nations." You would often hear comments such as, "Our neighbors are really good Christian people," meaning that they had integrity, kindness, generosity, respect for the law, and upright morals. They might not have had one speck of personal faith, but they would be called "good Christian people." Why? Because their behaviors and ethics exemplified Christlike nature. Most of the population at that time would have agreed that the Bible's standards of character were to be followed and celebrated. Sunday, in most families, was known as a day to honor God, and the real meaning of Christmas and Easter was well-known in society and highlighted in public schools, shops, and social groups as well as churches.

In Christian tradition, beliefs are based on an Almighty God who is perfect in love, purity, justice, wisdom, and truth. He is good and hates evil and defines these attributes and the behaviors of His nature in His "Manual for Life," the Holy Bible.

I was raised in a generation where for the most part godly family values and moral ethics were celebrated, but our post-war parents were looking to engage in freedoms they had not experienced during the Great Depression and the Second World War. More and more emphasis was given to pursuing personal dreams rather than protecting and nurturing the family; at the same time, less and less emphasis was placed on a personal faith in Christ and obedience to His word.

At one time the Bible was read regularly in homes and in schools, but in the '60s a shift took place and the Bible was no longer given its honorable place. By the '60s mothers were leaving the home to work in order to make extra family income, stores were open on Sundays, and God was put on the back shelf. A sexual revolution came through the hippy movement and traditional family and marriage values were opposed. It became acceptable to engage in sex prior to marriage and to have multiple sexual partners. The spiritual revolution ushered in the New Age at the same time and enticed many to leave traditional Christian beliefs and follow deceptive teachings. Individuals lost their peace, so they turned to drugs, and the drug revolution with marijuana and LSD enticed the younger generation. The door was opened to a banquet of recreational, mind-altering drugs in the coming decades. Within the next 25 years, everything escalated and a new acceptance of sexual, spiritual, family, and moral values gradually moved society far from the plumb line of God's nature and word.

Over 60 years have now passed since the revolutionary shifts in the 1960s, and we are in a spiritual crisis that is manifesting in escalated lawlessness, corruption, immorality, hatred, dishonor, perversion, murder of the unborn at any stage of pregnancy or delivery, organ trafficking, etc. A new code of enforced morals is not going to fix the issue. New laws or government reform will not bring the peace or the alignment needed. We must have a massive dose of "raw God" to bring an internal conviction to those under the veil of deception. We must have a Holy Revolution that will invade and dispel the darkness!

In the Welsh Revival in 1904-1905, the nation was transformed because the conviction of the Holy Spirit fell on the masses. When they received His visitation, their lives were changed. The most corrupt and lawless sinners followed Him and their lives came into divine order and wholeness. A young man named

Evan Roberts had a passion to see his nation turn to the Lord and as a result gave himself to relentless and enduring prayer for over eleven years prior to the Holy Spirit's outpouring. Many of his generation met for prayer on a continual basis and cried out to God. The revolt against the corrupt, lawless, immoral, and godless behaviors in the day was contended for in the prayer closet and God rewarded them openly. When the Spirit came in power, everything changed.

In the First and Second Great Awakenings we see shifts that aligned not only the church but society to sincere faith, godly morals, and societal justice. Charles Finney was only 29 years old when awakening came to his own life and then spread rapidly to the masses. Jonathan Edwards was only 38 years old when he delivered the famous sermon "Sinners in the Hands of an Angry God" that was used as a catalyst for the First Great Awakening. George Whitfield was only 26 years of age when he led revival meetings in America spreading the Awakening.

A Holy Revolution is not an event, although the coming revolution will be recorded in history. Holy Revolution is knowing the One who *is holy*, partaking of and manifesting His nature, speaking His word, and living in holy union with Him. This was the result of past awakenings and this will be the fruit of the coming move as well. God is not interested in an outward form of godliness but is longing for the manifestation of His holy nature through His own.

Jamie Lyn Wallnau has experienced an intense hunger to know God intimately and, as a result, desires to raise the bar of faith, true devotion, and morality within the church. When this is realized, reformation can influence society. She is passionately calling forth those who will believe with her—who will birth a holy revolution with her. God is calling forth a younger generation of "revolutionaries" whom He will empower as He did young Jeremiah:

> *See, I have this day set you over the nations and over the kingdoms, to root out and to pull down, to destroy and to throw down, to build and to plant* (Jeremiah 1:10 NKJV).

Holy Revolution is an appeal for believers and especially those of the younger generation to rise up in this hour and raise the bar. May all who read this book experience fresh hunger and thirst for *Him, His kingdom, and His righteousness!*

PATRICIA KING
Author, Christian Minister, Television Host

Chapter 1

THE NARROW PATH

I grew up in a church environment where we did not talk about miracles or Jesus being a friend to us today, where "controversial" scripture was not read from the pulpit, and where I thought the Holy Spirit was a Catholic thing. I also remember knowing there was so much more to Him than I was seeing. Deep down, I wanted all of Him but had no grid for what that really meant. This book is proof that God is real and can transform anyone's life. On the outside I was a kind and loving Christian girl. However, I was insecure, doubtful, prideful, judgmental, depressed, gluttonous, hurtful, filled with self-hate, drank more than I should have at times, and cussed because I thought it was funny.

Then Jesus came along and used the foolish things to confound everything I thought was right and to confirm that everything I longed for in Him was actually real. I have been liberated from my weaknesses over and over again and strengthened by Jesus alone. The word of God has transformed me, and as I behold Jesus in worship, prayer, and the word of God I am constantly transformed.

For those who are weary of the "charismatic" church streams or way of life, I totally understand. I used to judge the very people I run with now because I genuinely did not know any different. I am so glad that I laid down what I thought God was like to lean in and discover what He is actually like. The more I learn about Him the more I come to discover I know nothing compared to what I will know in ten years if I keep leaning in. It keeps me humble and desperate to know Him more.

The first time I felt the Lord tell me anything was when I was in college. He told me that I was going to be an author and speaker. It wasn't a casual moment for me. It felt huge and groundbreaking. You are holding the first word and book I ever received from the Lord, and I am so happy it's happening now and not in 2006 when He first shared that with me. He has changed my life forever, and I want to share with you how amazing it is that we get to be part of what God is doing on the earth through His holy revolution in the remnant He is raising up right now. One of the biggest encounters I have had with Him commissioned me deeper into the liberating lifestyle of being holy.

You are going to discover what God has done and what God wants to do in your own life. There is a generation God is gathering right now, and we get to be part of it. It costs everything to join the revolution of men and women whose lives revolve around the man Jesus and who are boldly going where no one has gone before and doing what no one has done before. So this book paints a picture of how you and I get to be part of it—if you choose to be. Before we dive into the encounter I want to share a few things with you.

A SETUP

God is coming and He is separating us. Even within the believers He is looking for those who are willing to lay down everything to walk in uncompromising holiness, love, and the fear of the Lord. He is looking for those like Abraham who will lay everything on the altar (including fear of man) to be more aware of His presence in our lives. He wants those who won't allow the world to taint their identity because we are so aware of how good our God is and how much of our lives He deserves. It is the path most difficult to take. It's narrow and it is very costly, but it leads to eternal life in Jesus Christ. So few find it. So few are willing to give God their everything so that they can gain everything.

The world hands us manipulation, deceit, and division if we are not careful. The American dream in itself is to become a successful business man or woman who can give to those around them and do more than their parents did. The fruit looks so good on this tree. I have tasted it myself, and while the temporary joys of success and money were great, outside of my true nature in Christ it led to depression and void and lost passion. Many times it is quite deceiving if we don't keep watering our hearts with the Spirit and feeding our hearts with the word. The tree of knowledge of good and evil is a common tree for even believers to continue to eat from. It is all many of us have known because it's all that was handed to us from those we have grown up around or because of the things we let in our eye gates and ear gates in media, entertainment, etc.

I'm convinced that there is a tree that has been planted for eternity in the hearts of God's people called the tree of life. Many of us have read about this tree in the book of Genesis. The enemy always shows up handsome, alluring, tempting, and as a great rhetorician. In a moment if we are not prepared, like Adam and Eve, we can give in to this temptation. When God created us, He said we were good. Everything He created He called good. Our inheritance in Jesus Christ is to live a life abundant in His goodness and all things good, to know He is good, we are good, and everything we do is good.

We have become his poetry, a re-created people that will fulfill the destiny he has given each of us, for we are joined to Jesus, the Anointed One. Even before we were born, God planned in advance our destiny and the good works we would do to fulfill it! (Ephesians 2:10 TPT)

We have a destiny that each of us was specifically designed to accomplish with God, which can only be found in Him. We have to stop pursuing dreams in our own strength and slapping His name to it like He is running alongside us. I know that sounds intense, but I have been on that road and it led to some self-inflicted and unnecessary pain. Yet He has a rhythm and timing of all things good on this earth that He longs to create alongside you and me. We cannot fulfill this good calling and these good works without the friendship and Lordship of our heavenly Father.

THE HOLY ONE

There is nothing like the presence of the Holy One. I have looked and I have searched, and in seasons when I was not rooted in relationship with Him and His word, I fell. Where I am today is a result of what Jesus has done to me—yes, to me and others. I am a victim of the blood of Jesus Christ, and because of it I am part of a holy revolution. He desires to ravish you with His loving-kindness and friendship. His blood truly speaks a better word than our own strength and goals. All your dreams are nothing compared to the real dreams He has for you. You, my friend, were called to live a life so much more incredible than you could possibly ask for or imagine. He always out-dreams us. However, we must first lose this life to gain the one we are called to fulfill for all of eternity.

On this journey I have had in pursuit of Jesus, I have seen measurable fruit. I am not who I was ten years ago, five years ago, a year ago, six months ago, etc. I am consistently becoming more pure and holy. I am consistently becoming more and more set apart for His glory and His goodness. The best part is, I am not trying to become any of these things. I just keep gazing into the heart and eyes of Jesus, and He is purifying me along the way. He has my whole heart. He can do with me and this life as He pleases. I get accused, I get laughed at, I get judged and criticized along the way. Jesus warns us about this in His word. It is worth it for me because I am laying it all down at His feet alongside my husband. The kingdom of heaven will be advanced and the very assignment and calling He has placed on our lives will be completely filled because we are in full pursuit of this man, Jesus.

> *Come to God through the narrow gate, because the wide gate and broad path is the way that leads to destruction—nearly everyone chooses that crowded road! The narrow gate and the difficult way leads to eternal life—so few even find it!* (Matthew 7:13-14 TPT)

I have wept and wept and wept over this scripture. I cannot believe that we could be so caught up and distracted by the ways of this world that we would ever be caught on the broad path that leads to destruction. The crazy part is that I have been on this path and most of us have been, are, and if we are not careful can be. Jesus says that nearly everyone chooses that crowded road. It's the narrow gate that is the difficult way, but it leads us to eternal life with Him. This is the core message in His word that I believe we carry on this earth, and I long to see us all take it together. There are painful and teachable moments of growth on this path and there are moments of others not understanding that come with it, but it is worth it because it is always with Jesus. The greatest part is that He knows what that feels like and how hard to make many decisions on this path are, because He came and walked this path too. Still, He chooses to walk close with us the whole way again and again and again.

THE ENCOUNTER

I went through an encounter with God that completely changed my life in April of 2017. I was directing a global conference at our church in Dallas and really encouraged our volunteers to work in excellence leading up to the conference, and to be surrendered to the Lord if He showed up during sessions. I told them we would be "Martharys." I would define "Martharys" as men and women who prepare a place for Jesus and others to dine, like Martha did, but when Jesus arrives they sit and eat with Him. Martha had a gift of hospitality, and we were going to serve with all of our hearts. Mary had a heart to sit at Jesus' feet and forgo everything else to do so. We would take both of these incredible women as examples and serve this way. If someone was working the T-shirt table and the Lord was opening a door for them to meet with Him, they had full permission to sit with the Lord. If someone got upset that the T-shirt table wasn't being manned while someone was encountering our Jesus, then we would be gracious for their personal deliverance. I am kidding; but seriously, these scenarios bring up a lot in people. Little did I know that I would be one of the people encountering Jesus in an unexpected way.

We had a session where someone had a word of knowledge for a woman named Sheila with flat feet to be healed. No one in the room immediately came to the front when the word of knowledge was mentioned. Then a young man said he had a friend who attended our church named Sheila, so he called her. When he called her (we put her on speaker phone over the mic), a young man at the front who had never prayed for healing for anyone before prayed for her. The funny part is that she was driving and had to pull over because she felt the burning in her feet. She looked down and said through a weeping voice of excitement and awe that arches had been formed in her feet.

I was amazed. Something was different about this healing for me. I had seen and heard about healings before, but I was in awe. Our heavenly Father healed someone's flat feet through the words of someone who had never prayed for healing for anyone before. Not only that, He did it through the speaker phone and into a microphone in a room full of people for someone who wasn't even in the room.

I was so blown away by what God did that I felt Him and His presence so unbelievably strong in that moment. It was overwhelming awe. I was sitting next to my boyfriend, who is now my husband, and knew what I was feeling could turn into a very emotional time with God if I gave in. In this moment, I felt Him present a choice to me. It was as if I could choose to lean into this moment with Him or get up and go direct the conference. If I leaned in, it was what I had been praying for everyone to experience, and if I just kept working I'd be giving up a moment I could never get back. In that moment I had no idea the impact my decision to "let go" would produce, but I chose to lean in.

I had so much faith for healing that I ran to find a man in the room whom I knew had cancer. Our church had been praying for his healing for several weeks at this point. I laid at his feet and just wept as the Lord showed me a few things that were really beautiful. I was wailing. This was not a pretty and delicate tear time with God. Nope. If you were in the room that held 600 people—you heard me. I was being shown things in heaven that words didn't even need to be said for me to understand. It was as if things were being revealed to me in a moment that were so supernatural and peaceful and so divine. I could see the cloud of witnesses and two men who have already passed away, looking at me and sharing the heart of heaven in that moment. They showed me how much more I had to learn in the revelations of heaven on earth. I wanted to know more, and it deposited a hunger in me. They also gave me information and insight that I will always treasure in my heart. When I was done weeping at this man's feet, I knew the Lord was not done. He presented to me a second time: "Do you want to keep directing the conference or do you want to see more?" After I saw what I had just seen I got up and ran to the back office area and continued to weep. During this whole time it was as if I was the only one in the room and all I could feel was the presence of heaven.

I lay on the floor as though there was heavy weight within me that glued my body to the cold concrete. I was unable to move for three hours. Yes, this even went into the next session time, and I am so thankful that people knew how to step in and help facilitate the conference. You see, there had been many people encountering the Lord in such powerful ways at our church in the weeks leading up to the conference. God was already doing supernatural things through leadership so that it was not unusual for something like this to happen. We had been experiencing a tangible presence of God in the room during our staff meetings. For those reading who may not know what I mean, it was like someone was standing behind us—when you can feel someone's presence. We could not see Him. However, we could feel Him in our meetings.

There was an understanding that this was God and it was good, so they just let me be so that the Lord could do what He wanted to do. I remember during the first part of the encounter I was trembling at the goodness of God. He was physically shaking anything and everything that was not holy out of me. I didn't even know what all of these things were; I just knew that's what was happening. His very presence in this encounter overwhelmed me to the point where I was no longer in the room where my body was lying. I was with my heavenly, sovereign, and divine Lord. I was in the presence of the Holy.

There was a moment when I saw Him take my heart out and give me a new one. He gave it to me whole, set apart, holy, and untainted. Completely new—in one moment, I had a new heart from Jesus Himself. Wow. Open heart surgery. He told me that I would need to water it with the Spirit and feed it with the word for it to stay as strong as it was when He placed it within me. A simple blueprint for wholeness.

As the encounter continued, I knew what He was doing in me was not just for me but for anyone who was willing to receive it. He revealed to me and allowed me to see people through His eyes. I was in a place of lightness. It was like a feeling of floating that would describe the beauty of His love. I could feel His pure, kind, and all-believing love for others. He does not look at us and see our imperfections with a notebook taking notes. No, He sees the beauty of our hearts and how

He created us to be, love, and do. Even writing about this time with God makes me giggly and in awe. I can feel the joy rising up from deep within me. He really loves us beyond anything we can possibly imagine.

My friend, you are so deeply loved by Jesus. He loves the pure-hearted wholeness that you were made in. He loves you as though you are perfect and blameless and desires to remind you of it daily. Sometimes, the world hands us such darkness that we forget how good we really are. I have a secret to share with you—you are doing much better than you think you are. He delights in every step you take and every move you make.

There were three women I remember coming into the room during this time I was with the Lord. Every time they came close to me He showed me how perfectly whole He created them to be. It was as if we had been so distracted by the tiny things in the world that we had each lost sight of how incredibly beautiful and powerful we are in Him. He was showing me how He loves us as though we had never sinned. If we could see ourselves the way Jesus loves us, our actions and belief system would be so shaken that we would be unstoppable forces of nature on earth from heaven. We would be exploding with love for people and it would be contagious. I knew that if we truly believed what He sees in us then we would walk like Jesus did on this earth with so much love and courage. Signs. Wonders.

Miracles. Many of us would be on different paths and careers and operating in deep wells of love for others.

One of the most life-changing things that happened to me in this encounter was when I started to hear, "Many are called but few choose. Many are called but few choose." I used to think this meant not everyone is called, which confused me. Only "many" are called, and from that many only a few choose Him. I had always hoped I was one of the called ones. However, what God meant by this shook me to my core. He switched it and began to say, "Everyone is called but few choose." Can we have a Selah moment here for like an hour? You mean that every single one of us is called but few of us choose? Wow.

I began to see people were presented with His goodness every single day in tiny ways. They were presented with His presence at church, and most denied Him each time because they were not willing to lose everything in that moment for fear of looking crazy. They would look at those crying out in the front, the ones who were truly giving Jesus everything, and judge them silently. They did not want to look "like that" and truly believed they did not need what that person was experiencing.

They had everything they needed. A strong business, a flourishing family, all the money they needed, a home, clothing, plenty of food, and they were happy showing up to church and slapping His name on their actions. However, what they didn't see was that if they were willing to choose Him in that very moment, if they were willing to lose everything right then, they would gain everything. I love what Patricia King says: "God plus nothing equals everything." It is so true. You don't have to believe this right now. You really don't have to believe this just yet. It will never change the truth behind this statement. If we have nothing but we have Jesus, my friend, we have everything. We cannot have this revelation without knowing Jesus.

The ones who were being presented with the presence of Jesus in these moments at church were so desensitized to these moments because they were in the habit of denying Him. They were front-row seaters. People of influence. People who had their lives together and said they were following the Lord. They were not truly giving Jesus their everything. If they lost all their earthly possessions, they'd be desperate and a hot mess. I began to weep. Each time I saw the faces of His beloved sons and daughters not wanting to lose it to gain everything, I wept. How could we not choose Him? Father, how could we not choose You? You are so good and everything You have is good. Your path leads to eternal life, but the paths of this world lead to destruction.

What are we doing if we aren't losing everything to gain everything? The scary part is most of us, when we are on this broad path, don't even know we are on the broad path. We become desensitized to the spiritual world and His presence in our lives every day. My hope and desire is to break down the revelations that the Lord has given to me to help us see and taste and know how good the narrow path is. I feel like God gave me a new toy in 2017 and let me discover it with Him. Now He is inviting me to share all of the beautiful details of this new toy He gave me with you. It was just a set of revelations in 2017, but now it is a way of life for me.

> *Come to God through the narrow gate, because the wide gate and broad path is the way that leads to destruction—nearly everyone chooses that crowded road! The narrow gate and the difficult way leads to eternal life—so few even find it!* (Matthew 7:13-14 TPT)

I desire people to choose the Lord, even if it looks crazy or scary when He comes. You know when that "one person" looks silly in service and the judgmental thoughts start coming in, like, "Wow, that's embarrassing" or "God, please don't come at me like that." The list goes on and on, but those thoughts alone can withhold an incredible moment. What if it is God and it's how He wants to touch your heart? What if that crazy moment could transform your hurt and pain into joy and wholeness forever? What if that one moment could unleash the dreams, desires, and hopes you have for your future and your family? Better yet, what if you letting go in that moment would reveal to you *His* dreams and desires for your future and your family?

TRUE RELIGION

Religion that God our Father accepts as pure and faultless is this: to look after orphans and widows in their distress and to keep oneself from being polluted by the world (James 1:27 NIV).

Oftentimes, those who keep themselves from being polluted by this world are judged and criticized deeply. I think of how God said in First Corinthians 1:27 that He uses the foolish things to confound the wise. There were so many times in the past when I was too wise to let the foolish and godly thing wreck me for the better. I judged and criticized others for looking ridiculous and making a scene, so I missed out on the better thing. I even see many Christians blame others for being "too religious" for not drinking alcohol, listening to certain music, or watching certain things on television. Do we not see a time when the things that represent true religion in the eyes of our Father are the things we must stop judging and start seeking understanding on?

Many who blame others for being religious are the ones wrapped and engulfed in the ways of this world themselves and have no idea. The discomfort of the real gospel can make those who feel comfortable very uncomfortable, and sometimes the only way to feel better about their comfort is to accuse or deny how someone else is choosing to live with God. Can anyone relate? I have been guilty of this myself. I am grateful we serve a God who is kind, and His kindness is what has led me time and time and time again to repentance. He longs for us to seek Him so that these things can be revealed to us along the way.

My life has changed drastically in so many ways, and ten years ago I would have told you the way I am living now is too extreme. Today, I can't escape my desire to love Jesus, and part of that is not doing things that grieve His heart or things that I genuinely don't think He would do with me. This all has come with conviction, and only the Spirit of God can bring this. Not the spirit of Jamie Lyn or the spirit of whatever else that might try whispering. If you feel a tug of change in your heart, don't delay—respond to that kind and loving voice within and watch how that ripple effect ignites a new way of life for you.

The warriors who will be part of the Holy Revolution won't justify their flesh to stay comfortable. This will be a generation that responds to the tiny tug in their gut called the Holy Spirit. This generation will say, "God, why are You tugging on me here? Tell me what to do and I will do it." Even if it means laying down something we have loved, loved, *loved* because we trust that what He is course-directing our time and affection to is far greater. We cannot live this way without knowing the man Jesus.

We are in a time when thousands are choosing to take this path with God. That's why He released me to share this with you now. It's time for us to see Him so we can know who we are and so that we can advance the kingdom of heaven on this earth—for eternity, together. There is a broad path that many of us have been on. Think about it—when the shaking comes in life and we are on the broad path, we start getting jolted up against those who are getting shaken alongside us. It's so crowded, and the discomfort of the crowding causes us to be at war with one another. Most people choose this path. When we choose the narrow path and the shaking comes, we are not bumping up against everyone. We are able to see that the foundation we are standing on is strong and eternal. We get to be the peacemakers on this road while everything around us is shaking. We are on the path that gets brighter and brighter for those walking in righteousness. We also get to invite others on this path with us. We get to disciple and pray in this massive harvest.

PRAYER FOR HOLINESS

Jesus, thank You for a clean and pure heart. I invite You to come clean house in my own heart. As I read this book, will You reveal to me what You desire me to know? I invite You to come into every crevice of my being to reveal who You are and who You say I am. I desire to encounter You, Father. Help me, Holy Spirit, to be one whom our Father finds on this path. I want You, Father, and I need You. Amen.

Chapter 2

HOLINESS

But now that you have been set free from sin and have become slaves of God, the benefit you reap leads to holiness, and the result is eternal life.
—ROMANS 6:22 NIV

The moment we give our lives to Jesus, we are set free from sin and become slaves of God. We get to serve the kindest and most generous King—the One who is high above anything in the entire universe because He made it all. We serve Him and obey Him, not because of legalities but because we are madly in love with Him. Those who give their lives over to holiness have found that this is the only way of truly knowing Jesus and walking in His ways. The benefit of a life free of sin is holiness, and the result of holiness is eternal life with Him in heaven. We want to be free from sin and we want to spend eternity with Him. Therefore, we must answer the call and honor of being set apart as holy sons and daughters.

HOLINESS ISN'T A BAD WORD

*For God did not call us to be impure, but to
live a holy life* (1 Thessalonians 4:7 NIV).

The word *holy* doesn't really rile a whole lot of
people up with excitement. I feel it's been abused
and misunderstood many times by the church. Many
people see it as a list of rules that we have to follow
in order to accomplish the checklist of holiness. Then
when they fail, it feels horrible and shameful and completely unattainable. Y'all, I wouldn't want to be a part
of that either. Holiness can only be found through relationship with the man Jesus.

In my journey with Him, holiness has come over
time. I used to walk in sin, and now I walk with the
Holy Spirit. This isn't a three-step program. It would
be easy to make it that. If we don't have a revelation of
His love for us, it's hard to be in relationship with Him.
It's easy to worship, pray, and read the word. None of
that will "make you holy." When you get to know the
character and nature of a person, you grow in trust
and love for them.

It's the same way with God. If we worship, read
the word, and pray as a law or checklist of items to do
because we are a Christian, we are missing the point.
God wants you to encounter Him while you do these
things. There is a passion and hunger that comes when
you discover the actual person of God. There are revelations and awe-inspiring moments that will come

in the places when your heart is burning before His throne. Holiness becomes a desire because it comes from such a deep place of love for Him that you don't want to do anything that isn't holy. Selah.

I grew up in a church, not a household, hearing "once a sinner always a sinner." There are many churches out there today that are sin-focused. That didn't make sense to me at a young age. I knew deep down that wasn't true because that would defeat the purpose of Jesus showing us how we can live. I grew up knowing God but not always knowing how to follow Him. Even so, I tried to become free by focusing on the sinful nature of depression, self-hatred, other people's mistakes, and gluttony. It got worse. Deep down I knew it was not the Lord's will for me to be walking in such darkness, but I read my Bible as law instead of love and did not hand Him these dark places. There came a time in my 20s when I really handed Jesus the darkness. I invited Him in as a friend and Lord because I was tired of experiencing the same thing over and over and over again. That changed everything for me.

How can a young man keep his way pure?
By guarding it according to your word
(Psalm 119:9 ESV).

The word of God teaches us how to keep the way pure and our hearts pure. When I began to read the word with the Holy Spirit and only take what He said about me as truth, I became a very skilled spiritual volleyball spiker. If a poopy thought came to me, I would spike it down and replace it with His word because I was getting filled with the word of God. Over time I got delivered, and now those things are not part of my battlefield. They are part of my history with God, but they have allowed me to become holy in thought and action. I share this because beholding Him and trusting Him has helped me grow and mature into one who desires, loves, and finds true liberty in living a life set apart with Him.

HOLINESS PROTECTS YOU

And a highway shall be there, and it shall be called the Way of Holiness; the unclean shall not pass over it. It shall belong to those who walk on the way; even if they are fools, they shall not go astray (Isaiah 35:8 ESV).

The highway of holiness is for the warriors who seek Jesus and destroy the works of the devil. This highway is protected and the unclean and ferocious beasts cannot walk on it, as mentioned in Isaiah 35. This highway is for all who live in the way of our God. When you dive into this passage, it says in verse 10:

They will enter Zion with singing; everlasting joy will crown their heads. Gladness and joy will overtake them, and sorrow and sighing will flee away (NIV).

Coming from a daughter who was delivered from depression, I would have to agree that holiness brings immense joy. I would also like to mention that I have been off of this highway, and I was getting taken out by the poopy ways of the enemy. The highway of holiness has liberated me from darkness and allowed me to be acutely aware of the presence of God in my everyday life.

It is essential to protect every side of our senses and every gate we have in order to stay on this highway. Evil cannot live with holiness. There can be no mixture here. After all, it is a choice to live this way with God or not. That choice alone is the kindness of our God. He did not want us to be puppets; He wanted us to experience His love from such a real place that we would choose to return that love to Him. It is a beautiful exchange.

NOT FOR THE MUNDANE

Many times I have heard people say that we cannot live like Jesus. No one can live up to those standards. I could never agree with that statement. After all, that contradicts the scriptures and the whole purpose of why Jesus came—to show us what is possible with God on earth. He commanded us to be holy as He is holy. Check it out:

> *But as he who called you is holy, you also be holy in all your conduct, since it is*

written, "You shall be holy, for I am holy"
(1 Peter 1:15-16 ESV).

This actually says to be holy in all of your conduct. In Second Corinthians it says to make every effort to be holy. Which means this road is not for the mundane, y'all. No, it is not for those who are looking for that giant red easy button either. It requires a rewiring of conduct and lifestyle. It requires us falling so madly in love with God and understanding how we can put trust in Him to be able to lay all of the fleshly desires at His throne of mercy and grace. When you become holy, you choose to die to all of the lusts of the flesh in order to live the life of eternal joy. This is a daily choice we all have and the fruit of it is knowing Jesus more and walking in His ways.

Make every effort to live in peace with everyone and to be holy; without holiness no one will see the Lord (Hebrews 12:14 NIV).

"Make every effort" really stands out to me in Hebrews 12:14. *Effort* in good ole Merriam-Webster's dictionary means "conscious exertion of power: hard work." That means it takes our own hard work to live in peace with others and to be holy. There are moments when I have had to work really hard to live in peace with people who accused me or criticized me. The fruit of it was peace (shocker), and it was another moment on the timeline that helped me grow and mature.

When I say "work really hard" I don't mean strive. I mean, instead of leaning on myself in my flesh, I submitted what I thought I should do for what God has called me to do. Sometimes, it takes more work to respond with God than to react in our flesh. Often, that requires obedience to what His word says until it becomes a natural instinct. Obedience is a beautiful thing to the Lord. It means we are doing what we know is holy rather than what our flesh and feelings desire in that moment.

Without holiness, we won't see the Lord. That is a pretty huge statement. I am willing to lay any dream or desire down if it would have kept me from seeing God. It is so easy to get distracted with all of the billboards of culture and life in this world. Many are very enticing, screaming to fulfill all lusts, and that comes as no surprise because so was satan. I mean, lucifer's beauty led him to pride, and if we are not rooted in righteousness we can get sucked into this ourselves. Holiness is displaying the beauty of our heavenly Father for all of eternity and seeing Him in every part of our journey.

> *Since we have these promises, beloved, let us cleanse ourselves from every defilement of body and spirit, bringing holiness to completion in the fear of God* (2 Corinthians 7:1 ESV).

When I look at how much my life has changed because of the leadership of the Holy Spirit, I know that I myself could not have protected my body and spirit from defilement. Jamie Lyn didn't flex her way into holiness. The blood of Jamie Lyn didn't wipe away her sins—no, only Jesus did. I know that because of my relationship with the Holy One and protecting my time internally and outwardly, He has made me holy. He has shown me what to cleanse myself of, and He even did it in a moment, in the encounter I shared with you in the first chapter. I literally cannot do what I used to do when it comes to drinking alcohol, watching certain shows or movies, speaking poorly about others, or listening to others speak poorly about them. He has shown me how to stay cleansed even in my mind because of His perfect fear—loving what He loves and hating what He hates. God hates the things that keep us from being close to Him and knowing Him. He desires us to be free and holy.

In my weakness, I can boast because He has made me holy. I have fallen so deeply in love with the Holy Spirit that I cannot imagine grieving Him. I have had moments when I knew I grieved Him. Moments when I did not listen to the tug of His voice. Now, I have tasted and seen and know that He is worth all of the sacrifices of a culture that does not reflect Him, to live in His reverent and holy fear.

RADICAL HOLINESS

What is holiness like for our generation? We are most definitely stepping into an hour where persecution is getting much heavier for those who stand and walk in true holiness. This invitation to live this way will cost you everything you have, but it will reveal the truth that everything we need will be found in Jesus. The world is deceptive. Our flesh is deceptive. Christ is not deceptive. We have the honor of following Him. He said it would not be easy, but you won't be apart from Jesus, and that is the ultimate gift of life fulfilled.

The difficult journey ahead and narrow road with God will become a delight of instruction, correction, and growth. Persecution and accusation will push us closer to the Lord, not further away. The enemy will have to watch as God Himself promotes the mighty men and women of God into high places for tearing down false idols in the land and for staying purely open to God alone. Tearing down idols in different spheres of influence will require wisdom, understanding, and an anchoring in Jesus alone.

Jesus was mocked, He was beaten, He was the most innocent and pure man who has ever lived and we will begin to take part in the suffering of living a set apart life. As unromantic as this sounds, there is something about laying on the floor weeping in the prayer room for the hearts of those who have persecuted you to know Jesus and be holy. There is something about humbling your heart before God and asking Him if there is truth behind the accusations because if there is, you don't want anything in you that keeps you from being pure. There is something about taking part in the suffering that Jesus experienced when He walked this beautiful earth for every single one of us, even those being mean.

Radical holiness will come when we realize that nothing we own on this earth matters compared to His great love. Nothing of true value can be taken from us because the greatest treasure we have on earth is Christ and eternal life with Him. There will be radical giving of homes, finances, time, resources, love, service and more that we get to pour out to those in need. There will be multiplication in our lives because of the way we steward what He has given us. Holy men and women will be seen in the streets of our nations with amazing innovations, wise ideas and solutions to the greatest problems. God invites us to be led by Him every single day and respond to His voice alone.

He lets us decide and choose which life we want to live. All in or all out. Because y'all know what He says about being lukewarm—He's going to spit them out. I don't want to be spit out by God. I have been lukewarm and it was miserable. Repentance brought me back to Him. Obedience kept me near Him even when I didn't feel like it. That obedience later turned to a relationship of love, admiration, and devotion to Him alone. My prayer is that the man Jesus will empower and inspire you to dive *all* in on this adventure.

I don't want to get to heaven and say, "Jesus, look what I did for You! I had three television shows and I said Your name every episode. I built a business that funded other dreams people had for You and I traveled the world telling people about You!" and then hear the Lord say, "But, Jamie, you didn't know Me. I wanted to do all of this *with* you." No. No. No. I want to get to heaven and hear Him say, "Well done, my good and faithful Jamie Lyn. I loved being creative and spending time with you." This journey of building with God will require relationship with Him and a daily walk of dying to our fleshly desires and living for the desires that are found in His heart.

Remember, as you look back at the encounter I had with the Lord—He took everything out of me that was not holy and replaced it with a perfect heart. He wants to do the same for all of us. All we need to do is water our heart with His Spirit and feed it with His word. Every action we take moving forward will come from this place.

HOLY DISRUPTORS

Some of the greatest reformers of history came in to disrupt the momentum that culture was riding that wasn't good. There are cycles that are turning and turning, and in order for light to invade the dark cycles it will require someone who is willing to come in and disrupt it. There are two different types of reformers who will keep showing up in history. There are those who make a positive change and there are those who do not. Men and women who make a positive change are filled with love and truth. They are the peacemakers

who are willing to stand up for what's right and biblical, even if it is costly. Then there are those who have
been deceived and are pushing agendas that lead to
destruction. Hitler and Jim Crow are extreme examples of this but they were able to convince a people
group that another was worthy of death when they
were innocent. Whether good or bad, these reformers
help shift an entire culture in families, cities, states,
businesses, nations and the earth.

You won't always be liked and loved by people if
you are truly being led by the Holy Spirit and speaking up about things that are important to Him. That's
when holiness kicks in and allows you to handle it like
the ultimate champion of heaven.

> "You must never be fearful about what you
> are doing when it is right."
> —ROSA PARKS

In a day of segregation, Rosa Parks was sitting on a
bus and something came over her and she realized in a
moment that she was going to take a stand by remaining seated right where she was. She even said, "I only
knew that, as I was being arrested, that it was the very
last time that I would ever ride in humiliation of this
kind." There were other disruptors who also spoke
up in action who came before her on the bus such as
Bayard Rustin, Irene Morgan, Lillie Mae Bradford,
and Sarah Louise Keys. Things have changed because
they empowered thousands more to stand against this

injustice, and it allowed veils to be removed from the eyes of people who couldn't see how dark things were. Rosa also fought on the front line with Martin Luther King, Jr. and others to continue to reform the gaps she saw in society. In this Holy Revolution, we cannot allow ourselves to have veils over our eyes that allow injustices to continue.

> "You may choose to look the other way, but you can never say again that you did not know."
> —WILLIAM WILBERFORCE

William Wilberforce was in parliament and became a born-again Christian. When this happened, the life-long reformer in him began to rise up. He fought for years to obliterate slavery in the British Empire. Three days before he died, he found out it was passed in parliament and 100 more people were evangelical Christians in parliament! He did much more than this, but imagine fighting to end slavery among men who normalized such a thing. He gathered all the resources he had to fight to end such a deep and dark injustice. What could God be calling you to fight for in our generation?

The areas you are called to disrupt and reform will not always be easy. It will require endurance to keep pushing through and seeking God for wisdom on how to partner with Him in His victory. He is with you and He will fight for you. All we need is to be willing to stand in our convictions that are holy and not allow the world to influence us in ways that keep us from accomplishing the work God has set before us.

These people fought long and hard as influencers in their day and did much more than these two examples. Many in our generation will be influencers in all different spheres. You may be called to disrupt the world with movements of worship, prayer, business, fashion, arts, entertainment, media, education, medicine, family, revival, social justice, government, and more. Whether the world knows our name or not in these battles ahead, we must learn to live a life set apart so that when we step into these places we do it with pure radiance and no compromise.

PRAYER FOR HOLINESS

Jesus, thank You for Your leadership. Spirit of God, I ask for You to make me more aware of the nudges of conviction so that I can lay down everything that keeps me from knowing You more. Would You stir desire in me, Holy One, to be holy as You are holy? Would You help me walk courageously toward You and with You? I repent for every time You have tried to get my attention and I have ignored You to please my flesh. I want to be led by You, Jesus. I desire to lay down everything in my life that keeps me from walking in holiness with You. Thank You for Your love. Amen.

Chapter 3

THE MODERN-DAY BATTLE

In their case the god of this world has blinded the minds of the unbelievers, to keep them from seeing the light of the gospel of the glory of Christ, who is the image of God.
—2 CORINTHIANS 4:4 ESV

The world is shouting while heaven is whispering. We are facing a modern-day battle of light and darkness with technology, culture, music, fashion, podcasts, books, shows, movies, fame, influencers, government, and more. If we don't accept His invitation to live holy, these platforms can distract us from being able to walk and live a life set apart that God deeply longs for us to walk in. I had a friend tell me once on the phone, "If the enemy can't get you to sin, he will try to keep you distracted."

Christian, if you claim to be one, then you need to be ready to put the armor of heaven on and take back the holy ground we have lost to evil because it's time to build with God. We must lean into the whisper of heaven and remain there so that when the shouting of the world rises more and more, we can clearly sense what our heavenly Father is saying and doing.

When you see Him, you cannot help but give Him every single thing you have and want. In return, He will hand you what was meant for you to have all along. When He reveals the things we have been deceived by, He doesn't do it to shame us. He does it because He loves us so much, and those very things are keeping us from seeing the full truth that can only be found in an untainted vessel. These are a few distractions that can taint our hearts and lenses if not watchful. I know there are many more; these are the few I felt led to highlight.

CULTURE SETTING

Do not love the world or the things in the world. If anyone loves the world, the love of the Father is not in him. For all that is in the world—the desires of the flesh and the desires of the eyes and pride of life—is not from the Father but is from the world. And the world is passing away along with its desires, but whoever does the will of God abides forever (1 John 2:15-17 ESV).

The world is setting the tone and has been normalizing divorce, abortion, slander, betrayal, homosexuality, lukewarm Christianity, lust, perversion, depression, gender confusion, dark music, pornography, drunkenness, witchcraft, and more. When we let these things into our eye or ear gates, even in subtle ways, we are agreeing with them on some level. When you are madly in love with the Father, the worldly lusts become distasteful and irrelevant to you and your baseline of living. When you fall madly in love with God, you cannot help but say "no" to the world, and you desire to create purely with Him. This is all about walking in relationship with Jesus day in and day out. He is our holy discipler and teacher now. Oftentimes the world can seem desirable because it markets to every place of our weak flesh that wants more in that area. When you are being led by the Holy Spirit, whom He gifted us all with, He will reveal to you what is okay and what isn't as you continue to walk in holiness.

> *You are the light of the world. A town built on a hill cannot be hidden. Neither do people light a lamp and put it under a bowl. Instead they put it on its stand, and it gives light to everyone in the house. In the same way, let your light shine before others, that they may see your good deeds and glorify your Father in heaven* (Matthew 5:14-16 NIV).

We have been called the light of the world. This means we are the ones lighting up the world with the innovations of heaven in serious excellence. We can be the ones setting the tone for culture carrying the solutions. We can be the ones marketing such life-giving content that it obliterates any false idol. Many believers go into different spheres of influence and get caught up in deception because they don't stay on the narrow path of uncompromising holiness. I 1,000 percent believe it is possible to be a powerful musician, businessman, educator, parent, or actor today and not compromise. It will require a lot of sacrifice, excellence, and a heart burning for Jesus along the way.

BYE BYE, FEAR

I know this sounds intense, but eleven out of the twelve disciples were martyred. I can't just casually say that and keep going. They were martyred because they were willing to put themselves in harm's way for others to know the man Jesus, whom they literally walked this earth with. That's pretty crazy.

In America, we are nowhere near facing that level of persecution. In the States it's only our reputation with the world's culture that gets put on the line. Yet so many of us are afraid to stand up for what's righteous when the world disagrees. Fear to disagree when someone is being talked about poorly; fear to speak up about injustice and take action because man may come at us; fear to post about Jesus because our following may not approve; fear to stop listening to certain music or watching certain shows. Many of us can fill in the blank here with another moment we face daily. But we have bigger fish to fry here.

We have leaders influencing education who are fighting for children to be able to make a sex change at the age of eight years old. We have leaders who are wanting to normalize children choosing what sex they believe they are rather than helping them embrace the man or woman they were truly born to be. We have children being trafficked and their bodies being sold 20 times a day, even within our cities. We have the innocent blood of babies being shed, and all of this has happened because we allowed evil men and women to change the laws, rules, and regulations. This is not the government's job to fix; it is the body of Christ going into all the world and making disciples. We cannot be afraid to speak up so we can stand for holiness and be the voice of heaven on earth.

I met a man recently who did some serious secret ops for the United States military. He had the highest clearance and was even above the Navy Seals. I was telling him how cool I think he is and how much I love learning about the Navy Seals and those who are the real-life superheroes. He said watching shows about it is more scary than when he was in it. It was such a part of his normal life that while he was running into these special operations for our country, he wasn't afraid. I feel this kind of courage will become normal for the warriors in the holy revolution. When we know who we are, who our Commander of heaven is, and what the job is, we are able to be more courageous in all that we do.

My friends go into some of the darkest places of the earth sharing the gospel. I love the Dawkins family. Robby has been put in prison overseas a few times now for sharing the gospel. He says that he feels fear, but because of his love for Jesus it compels him to keep moving forward to bring salvation to those who do not yet know our Savior. Can you imagine this kind of courage in our own personal lives?

One of the hardest countries to minister in is America because it is thriving in the natural. Many people have what they need and don't feel the necessity of leaning on Jesus and being led by Him. This is why we must have courage and be ready to share the gospel in every sphere of influence. Especially us creative ones. I love this verse:

> But in your hearts revere Christ as Lord. Always be prepared to give an answer to everyone who asks you to give the reason for the hope that you have. But do this with gentleness and respect (1 Peter 3:15 NIV).

We have the honor of preparing a way for the return of the Lord. We can do this by replacing evil with good. Holiness is tearing down false gods and idols, then replacing it with truth, righteousness, and purity. This path is filled with moments when we could have ignored our gut instinct to do the God thing, but we chose the God thing over and over and over again. It's when we die to the cries of our flesh every day to say "yes" to our Savior. It is a daily sacrifice to walk in His ways on this earth. We have many battles ahead, but while we live through them and when we come out on the other side stronger, we must worship and point others to Jesus, always.

He is at the beginning, in the midst, and at the end of this revolution. He isn't sending us off alone. He doesn't ask us to do something He has not already done. He is with us through His Holy Spirit, and many times He is with us through one another. We get to lean into Him in our weakness. We get to bring others in to help do what we cannot do on our own. The Holy Spirit is leading us every step of the way—when we submit to Him. The *choice* God gave us to live this life or settle in comfortable apathy is truly one of the most beautiful gifts.

INFLUENCER GENERATION

It is more than okay to be an influencer. In fact, you are an influencer. We also read about them daily in our Bibles. But those men and women were influenced by God, and I have a hard time believing they knew they'd go down in one of the greatest history books of all time. Today our greatest influencer is named Jesus.

We are living in an age when anyone can build a platform on social media with zero accountability. This comes with great responsibility. When I was younger, social media did not exist. I still remember the computer booting up for several minutes, and no one knew to be impatient. Technology has evolved so quickly that if it takes more than three seconds for a screen to load, there can be a twinge of impatience and many exit off the screen. Listen, we received invitations to birthday parties in the mail with printed directions on them. Some of these invitations were just hand written. Cell phones were not a thing yet. We had friends when I was little, not cell phones.

In 2011, I did my thesis in graduate school on the benefits of cellular mobile devices in the classroom, deriving from the students' perspective because it was such a new and cutting-edge topic. It's evolved so much that my thesis could be thrown out the window at this point. This is crazy! If you were invited to speak somewhere when I was younger, it was because of your knowledge and expertise in a particular subject.

Now, anyone can build a platform and all of us are on the front line discovering this new wave of technology and social media that other generations did not have to battle. Creativity, studies, and technology are evolving at our fingertips so quickly that it's easy for anyone to jump on and "ride the momentum" of change without one thought as to who is leading the momentum.

It is not a small task to have thousands of people following you and watching you. Anyone can open up a social media account, create a cool aesthetic, be consistent, and do all of the step-by-step things to build a following. Who or what are all of these followers being led to? Because whatever spirit you're operating in is what you're drawing them to and that spirit may not always be holy. We are called to do what we see the Father doing and say what we hear the Father saying. So much easier said than done. It's why God sent us the Holy Spirit, and He only shares with us what the Father is saying.

Influencers will often battle the shouting of the world: "I want to be loved, I want to be seen, I want an increase in the number of followers on my social media, I want more people to like my posts, and I don't want to stir waters with people because I don't want to cause any hate in response." The thoughts of comparison can even come in, with your mind tempting you to compare your influence to someone else. These thoughts have come to me in my journey of media, and that's when I stop and engage the Holy Spirit. I do not take any action from a spirit of comparison or desire to be seen or known. I allow the Holy Spirit to lead me, and when I can feel He is leading me again, I move forward as He shows me. It's what you do when these thoughts come that help us grow. We can either lean into the Holy Spirit as our leader or work things out in our flesh and allow the world to lead us.

The greatest influencers in this generation will be the ones who know they are a child of God and that they have full access to their inheritance in heaven. Access to wild creativity, to abundance of resources to accomplish plans, solutions that will break chains of bondage, social injustice, and more!

CHURCH INFLUENCE AND FAME

Anyone who runs ahead and does not continue in the teaching of Christ does not have God; whoever continues in the teaching has both the Father and the Son (2 John 1:9 NIV).

There are many church influencers who are running ahead of God and not continuing the teaching of Christ; therefore, they do not have God. One of the dangers of desiring to be a public figure, even within the church, can come when we think we should be there before we are ready. There comes a time when you're really ready and you realize what you always dreamed about being or doing is actually a sacrificial call and comes with none of the fun bells and whistles that you thought it would. Why? Because our job in the church is not to have everyone love us and be well known. Our job is to be obedient to the spoken and written words of Jesus, to make room for the Holy Spirit to really come into the room as the leader and introduce people to Jesus. Our job is not to make sure everyone likes us, follows us on social media, and hears what we have to say while we are leading them. We do not transform people's lives. The presence of God does. Not everyone likes the sound of getting out of their comfort zone to truly live for Him. Not everyone is willing to live the life Christ preached about when no one is around. However, this is the only way for our hearts to remain pure as we lead people to Jesus.

I know that this may sound super harsh, and if you know me you know I deeply love the church. This is part of choosing to be in this Holy Revolution. It is being a living and breathing example of it so that when rubber meets the road, we are able to be exactly who God says we are and nothing less.

Many Christians of today's world have become so comfortable recreating what they have seen others do instead of getting in the habit of hearing the voice of God and obeying it.

Look at how broad the path is and remember that so few choose the narrow one—the path that leads to losing all of the selfish desires and temptations to instead follow the voice in the wilderness that longs to meet with us. This place in the wilderness is a place where we find the voice of God, and character is forged in this hidden place. It's the place where heaven is whispering and preparing us to be who God created us to be. It's the place many Christians preach about but not all choose to live in. It's the place where true transformation comes and we see who He is. Transformation and good fruit will always be a byproduct of a job well done in the desert and character-building seasons.

One problem is that the world operates in a wisdom that is contrary to heaven's wisdom. We need to be ready, because if we do not know the word, we will mistake the wisdom of the world for the wisdom of heaven. Satan comes with the flashy and pretty and handsome things, and we must be watchful and aware not to draw people to those things. These flashy church lights and smoke machines can even conjure up emotions that feel holy, but really it's just because the experience is cool.

If a rocket ship were taking off and the direction of the ship were off by a few degrees, they would eventually miss their target and their goal. When we agree with the small temptations and we don't lean into the hidden places with God, it puts us off course. I know this sounds extreme, and that's because this is very serious. We cannot afford to be deceived by the wisdom of the world. The wisdom of the world put Jesus on the cross because the religious leaders were expecting the Messiah to come much differently than He did. They also liked being the ones the church turned to for answers rather than God. In First Corinthians 2:9 it says that no eye has seen, no ear has heard, and no mind has conceived the plans God has for them, but it has been revealed by the Holy Spirit. We have the gift of the Holy Spirit to lead us into all truth. What an incredible friend, teacher, leader, comforter, and mentor.

I want to encourage you to ask the Holy Spirit to continue to reveal the motives in your heart when it comes to serving in the church or desiring a microphone or platform of any kind within it. Our call is to minister to the heart of Jesus when we gather together and disciple one another to go out into the world with uncompromising character and faith. People will not be transformed by who we are. They will only be transformed and set free when they meet the resurrector who lives within us and transforms us. Our joy is to introduce the lost, the weary, the wealthy, the widows, the orphans, the homeless, the most influential, etc. to Jesus. He should be the ultimate influencer in the body of Christ. That's why we are called the body of Christ. Not the body of (insert your name here).

KEEPING WATCH

Unless the Lord watches over the city, the guards stand watch in vain (Psalm 127:1b NIV).

The modern-day battle we are in today is one in which we must learn to keep watch over what we are letting into our gates. However, if we are watching our own house instead of letting the Holy Spirit do it, then we are watching in vain. How many times have we tried to overcome, but we failed because we didn't call upon our greatest helper? One of my favorite things is watching Him reveal to me how to keep watch because

He goes before and meticulously shows me how my actions are a reflection of what I have let in.

One of the biggest transformations I have seen is how I cannot watch movies or shows I used to watch years ago because I am no longer the lord of what I watch, Jesus is. He takes me in such deep places that I have learned that if He wouldn't select the show or movie, I won't either. The crazy part is, I have noticed this over time as fruit in my life. It did not happen in a quick moment.

Not too long ago I was watching a show that I thought was really pure. I loved the main characters and it was so lovely how pure they were and how they waited until marriage to be together. I laid down one night and felt a really dark and lustful spirit come at me. I couldn't see an image but had this strange feeling and wondered if maybe my husband was struggling with something lustful. We are very open with one another, so I went and asked him the next morning. I told him what I saw and what I felt and asked him if he was okay. He told me everything was fine and that he noticed there was a character in the show who had an inappropriate and sexual lifestyle. When I was watching this show, I had felt a small tug to turn it off when that character appeared the way he did, and I didn't obey it. Once I realized that, I immediately stopped watching the show and that thing never came back. Even though I loved that show so much, I gave that up *real* quick in order to make sure there were no unnecessary open doors in my life that did not lead to Jesus. I liked the show, but I love God way too much to allow that into my heart.

Many women have approached me about struggling with pornography. They were watching shows that had sexual promiscuity in them and lustful spirits. These shows had young adults sleeping together, pornographic-type scenes, and more. They had become desensitized to the darkness in it because they were watching pornography. Every time they watched these shows or movies it kept the door of lust open so the enemy could keep knocking, and they had no strength to rely on but their own. Now, for those who are inviting Him into their places of weakness, He helps strengthen them so that they are not facing these temptations alone anymore. This can only happen when we connect with a place of knowing these vile things grieve the Holy Spirit. He shows us how to say "no" to temptations that face us and protect our hearts because Jesus did that every day He walked this earth.

> *No temptation has overtaken you that is not common to man. God is faithful, and he will not let you be tempted beyond your ability, but with the temptation he will also provide the way of escape, that you may be able to endure it* (1 Corinthians 10:13 ESV).

God always provides an escape for us when temptation presents itself. So many times throughout the day we are faced with moments that lead to life or destruction. It could be saying "no more" to judgmental thoughts, romance novels, overdrinking, unhealthy eating, gossip, manipulative business moves, certain fashion trends, invitations in relationships that cross a line sexually, the movie your friends want to watch, certain media outlets, and I could keep going. These things add up over time, and I am so grateful we have a God who says, "I have an escape plan for you," no matter what temptations are coming our way. It always requires wisdom and courage to *choose* the escape plan. We can ask the Holy Spirit what we are letting in that could be keeping us from fully abiding in Him.

What social media influencers or friends are we following who rile up fear, self-hatred, jealousy, eating disorders, lust, greed, envy, doubt, fear, or more?

It is more than okay to unfollow someone who is too hard for you to be following. It's called the narrow path. I love the way my friend Lorisa Miller shared on this topic as she preached. She said she doesn't follow people on social media whom she isn't in relationship with. It keeps any of those unnecessary temptations of the mind from coming up, because she knows the people she is following personally. When you are walking in relationship with someone, it's much harder to feel those things come up within ourselves because we know more than their highlight reel and are cheering them on in their lives. I have taken this advice by really gauging who I should be following or not and how much time I should be putting to media.

CONTENT COMPASS

For God did not call us to be impure, but to live a holy life (1 Thessalonians 4:7 NIV).

Podcasts have become more popular as well as network marketing companies and the next big book release from a beloved author. These things can be absolutely wonderful and these things can be absolutely toxic. I have learned a lot here by making mistakes and want to share some insight with you. You have a compass within you called conviction from the Holy Spirit, and this compass is a really good tool in life.

If you are consuming any content that is causing you to put money first, unhealthy overtime to hit goals first, business first—I would say that's a red flag. If any of these things are teaching you to put them before you seek first the kingdom of heaven and His righteousness, I would step away. I know that's intense advice, but if these men and women you're listening to have it backward, you are letting that into you and it will affect you.

There are business men and women who will give great advice, and this advice is great to implement in our own lives, but it is most helpful when we filter it through the Holy Spirit. Many times I have been given advice from men and women in leadership, and when I brought it to the Holy Spirit I felt a no. I did this with humility knowing it might be a yes and it might be a no and really desiring His leadership. So before you make a deal or get involved with a new influencer, ask the Holy Spirit. I am not saying that if you work in finance you should not learn more about finance. I am not saying that if you're in a business and you need to know how to grow it that you can't find something out there to help you. God can teach us anything through anyone. It's just a really great habit to check in with the Holy Spirit to make sure all is okay with those we are listening to.

Content that will help us grow in our craft all boils down to one thing and that's being led by the Holy Spirit. Start trusting your gut. Start being faithful in those tiny nudges you're getting from Him, and you will be more than okay. I have had times in life when I ignored that nudge and then really wished I would have listened. It involved me repenting and cleaning up my mess. So trust first our heavenly leader. No business deal is worth grieving the heart of our heavenly Father. The more you trust Him in the small things, the easier it is to not be desensitized to heaven on earth.

There have been many times when leaders in my life did not feel conviction on something that I felt conviction on. Some people have accused me of being "religious." I understand because I used to be the same way they are. Many times living a life of conviction can look like legalism to others when really it's a deep love in your heart for Jesus. It can grieve my heart, but it helps me know how to pray for them. Never take advice that goes against your conviction. Even if they are believers, trust the beautiful conviction of the Holy Spirit. It is a great compass in our life.

My husband and I do not drink alcohol. We are not judging others who do. We are being led by the Holy Spirit and trusting His leadership in this area of our lives. Over time He took that desire from both of us and we have followed it ever since. We may not fully understand the "why," but we do fully trust Him. So we submit to Him in all that He is revealing to us.

Sometimes, you paying attention to your gut and submitting it to your leaders will help them grow. I have experienced this before and was grateful for the courage and their humility. It's a beautiful display of true leadership.

In summary of this modern-day battle that we are in, I want to encourage you to take the time to fall in love with Jesus. It requires pursuit on our end. Pursuit of the word and pursuit of Him in prayer. Pursuit of being patient until you fall in love with Him. When you do this, you can't help but make Him Lord of every decision you make. Being led by the Holy Spirit is an honor. I will be saying that a million times more in this book. He is the gift Jesus sent us to navigate the storms and battles we face every day on earth. He is a phenomenal TV guide, fashion guide, music guide, pastoral guide, book review guide, life coach, and to know Him is to love Him. The world cannot taint us if Jesus is truly first in our hearts.

PRAYER FOR MODERN-DAY BATTLE

Jesus, thank You for Your leadership. Thank You for showing me if there is anything I am building apart from You. Lord, if there is anything I am participating in or letting into my body, soul or spirit that I should not be, please reveal it to me. Thank You for helping me protect my gates. Show me, Holy Spirit, what You want to build together and help me walk through the hidden places and wilderness seasons with You. Amen.

Chapter 4

THE WATER

MY BEST FRIEND

I have to tell you about my best friend. I would say this is the deepest friendship I have ever had in my whole life. There were many moments when I was so broken that I couldn't see how much he was there for me, yet looking back I see he loved me really well through it. There were other times in my darkest hours when he was the only one whom I felt I could let into the darkest places of my soul. I was so depressed that I could hardly talk about it, yet he would always listen by just being present. He has consistently pointed me to Jesus, and there were times when I felt too broken to hear him. Somehow, he kept being patient with me.

I used to judge him pretty hard core, and when I did, he met me with forgiveness. I was really critical of him in my head because I didn't know him that well and was really good at judging from the outside. I am so glad I grew to know him and that those critical thoughts were demolished. I even judged others and he was quick to correct me. He is the kind of friend you pray for and dream of having. At least, I have always prayed for the kind of friend who shoots you straight with truth even if it isn't what I want to hear. Somehow, that kind of courage is rare, but this friend has never shrunk back.

He has trusted me with his secrets and he has never let me down. He has never broken my trust either. I have not always been faithful to him. He has always been faithful to me. He has always known how to comfort me when I was devastated, which taught me how to comfort others. He has waited for me patiently to choose love in places that were difficult, and he has brought me the most immense joy. None of this could have happened if he would have walked away from me when times were hard. He has taught me to be a faithful, honoring, and trustworthy friend. No matter what season he is in or I am in, he has never been shaken.

Yes, he gets even better, and I could keep going. His creativity is absolutely insane and innovative. He has openly given me ideas, and I cannot help but give him the credit for them. You've definitely heard me talk of this friend before if you follow any of my media outlets. The way he communicates to me about our Jesus is unbelievable. There is no other orator like him on planet earth. His leadership has blown me away, and one day I would be honored to lead and serve like him.

If you haven't caught on by now, this honored guest and this best friend of mine is the Holy Spirit. To be able to personalize such a friendship is otherworldly. Jesus sent us the perfect Friend. I can't help but weep as I write this. I love You, Holy Spirit. Thank You for being You.

The wonderful part is that Jesus gifted every single one of us with this incredible friendship. I look back at how present He was in all of the places and spaces I have gone, and He has never left me. Every single battle I faced *with* Him was won. He is my "plus one" everywhere and, my oh my, has He helped me grow and mature in some of the most unique situations and friendships. I desire every single one of us to be filled with the Holy Spirit. To be led by the Holy Spirit is the game changer of every single part of your life. I'd like to share my story with you, and I know you have your own with Him or maybe you'll have yours by the end of the chapter.

"WATER YOUR HEART WITH MY SPIRIT"

During the encounter I shared in the first chapter, the two main ingredients He shared with me were "water your heart with the Spirit and feed your heart with the word." When I heard this about watering with the Spirit, I knew it was to walk intimately with Him every day of my life. There are many ways we can do this that I will lay out in the next few chapters. When the Lord throws you down with His love on the floor for three hours and gives you a simple equation to keep your heart pure, you might as well listen and take to heart what He says, because it is probably important. These are game changers in this holy revolution and will transform every part of our life from the inside out.

This relationship gets to be super authentic and real for each one of us on a personal level. In order to water our hearts with the Spirit, we can discover this friendship with God in so many creative and wonderful ways. He will always reveal more of Himself to us as we continue to seek Him.

THE BAPTISM OF THE HOLY SPIRIT

If I were to encourage others to know their call, to get deliverance, to be set free, to grow in gifts, or to seek counsel, I would first empower them to learn the presence of the Holy One. The Holy Spirit leads us to Jesus and Jesus leads us to the Father and let me tell you— the answer is right here. Experiencing the tangible presence of the Holy Spirit is transformative.

When I was in college, my mom would call me and tell me about all of these amazing Bible studies she was attending at IHOP. Several phone calls later, I realized she was talking about International House of Prayer and not the pancake place. It was a hysterical moment of realization. I had gone to a few evenings with my mom where charismatic people were gathering, and though I thought it was crazy I also felt it was home. I received my first prophetic words from people at IHOP when I went for a conference and fell in love with Misty Edwards and the purity of her life. She made me feel normal, but also helped me see how much more I could experience in the Lord.

As I slowly had these introductions to the Holy Spirit in these places, I went on a prophetic art retreat with my mother. She really wanted to go and felt like this was something I was supposed to go to with her. On our way to this retreat, we passed through a place that had to do with the biggest fear I had carried for 18 or so years. This fear was so big that I wouldn't even say it in my mind because I didn't want the enemy to know what it was, even though satan cannot read my thoughts. Anyway, we drove to this gorgeous lake house in Georgia with Janice VanCronkhite as our lovely host and learned about prophetic art. Now, I was so excited to be there, but I felt quite shut down. As outgoing and bubbly as my personality is, I felt just monotone and strange.

One evening, we were sitting around the dinner table and there were about ten of us enjoying conversation and getting to know one another. My mom had always said, "Don't say your biggest fear out loud or the enemy can use it against you." I took that very seriously because I really didn't want to be around this fear in any capacity. So I asked my mom why she had told us that growing up. It was a funny moment because her response was, "Well, I don't know, Jamie. I guess I was always told that."

So the table had a conversation about this and Janice said, "Sounds like the enemy is using it against you because you're not able to say it." That was a Selah moment for sure. For the first time, I had the courage to share with the table what my biggest fear was. I told them it was dead bodies. I know it's silly but that's what it was. I remember shaking and sweating as I said it out loud. I was getting delivered. Then they asked me if I was baptized in the Holy Spirit and I knew I wasn't yet.

> *For by one Spirit we were all baptized into one body, whether Jews or Greeks, whether slaves or free, and we were all made to drink of one Spirit* (1 Corinthians 12:13 NASB).

These women surrounded me to pray, and I felt light come into my body and extract all darkness. I could hear screeching and squealing leaving the house as something powerful carried it out to be dealt with. I did not even know I had been carrying around darkness until light overcame my body. The one thing all of humanity was created to drink from was filling my body and I was getting really hydrated. My heart was being watered.

All of a sudden, I began to prophesy and give words of knowledge to the women in the room—words I could not have known had I not been baptized in the Holy Spirit. They encouraged me to pray in the Spirit, which was a stretch for me because my mind was really fighting how real that part of my life would be because of my religious upbringing. The language was right at the tip of my tongue if only I would let it out. The baptism of the Holy Spirit is an absolute gift and treasure. It's like the voice I had been hearing in my mind my whole life had a name and I was honored to grow in friendship with Him.

Every time I feel the presence of the Holy One, I am transformed even more into the likeness of Jesus. There is something about His presence that changes everything. I have been delivered from fears, from endometriosis, depression, gluttony, self-hatred, external and internal judgment, criticism, comparison, envy, doubt, and more. I have been able to hear the voice of our Father for others and see, hear, and understand the amazing plans God has for us. I have been able to discern situations that needed love and protection to come into place. All of these happen and more because of the baptism of the Holy Spirit. It is crucial that we make sure believers are baptized in the Holy Spirit. What a gift we have in this eternal friendship.

POURING OUT

I have set you an example that you should do as I have done for you (John 13:15 NIV).

Now that we have witnessed and experienced the presence, miracles, and love of the Holy Spirit, we can pour out for others. His Spirit empowers us to raise the dead, heal the sick, and to preach the gospel. I had no idea growing up that Jesus wanted us to be made whole. I thought that when people got sick that was possibly the will of the Father. This little ole Church of Christ girl who thought the Holy Spirit was a Catholic thing has been healed, seen blind eyes open, deaf ears open, the mute speak, people get delivered and healed, and lives so steeped in sin totally turn around into their full inheritance with God. I have not personally experienced the dead being raised yet, but if it was my biggest fear then I am sure it will be one of the greatest miracles I see in my life.

Jesus literally came and did all of these signs and wonders so that we could see and live heaven on earth. That same Spirit that raised Jesus from the dead is the very gift that Jesus sent to us because He knew it would be greater for us to have His Holy Spirit than for us to watch Him being the one doing it all the time. His Spirit empowers us to walk in these miracles as He did.

> All this I have spoken while still with you. But the Advocate, the Holy Spirit, whom the Father will send in my name, will teach you all things and will remind you of everything I have said to you (John 14:25-26 NIV).

Remember above when I was telling you about my best friend? I know all of this about Him because of the time we have spent together. Being around the very nature and presence of the Holy Spirit will transform you. When you see how the Holy Spirit serves you and leads you, you will know how to serve and lead others. When you experience His love, you will know how to love. When you experience His grace, you can extend grace. When you experience His mercy that triumphs over judgment, you will be able to extend mercy before judgment toward others. He literally teaches us by us watching and listening to Him.

There are things I believe God put within our very hearts that were designed uniquely for each of us during this time. I believe He gifted us the Holy Spirit to lead us in discovering this path and for us to experience friendship with Him. When I read the word and I am in a sticky situation where conviction comes up, the Holy Spirit reminds me what the word of God says and who God says I am. This empowers me to be holy and walk in righteousness. The Holy Spirit shows up in moments when I know that Jamie Lyn would not have reacted or responded that way. Nope, I know it was the Holy Spirit leading and teaching me in those moments.

THE FRUITS OF THE HOLY SPIRIT

But the fruit of the Spirit is love, joy, peace, forbearance, kindness, goodness, faithfulness, gentleness and self-control. Against such things there is no law (Galatians 5:22-23 NIV).

Fruit in people's lives helps us measure where they really are in heart and in spirit. It reveals what each person finds valuable in life, because you know how that saying goes, "We make time for what we value." We cannot help but let out what we let in. When you spend a lot of time with someone, you start taking on their mannerisms, sayings, or changing your behaviors because you're learning new ones. It's the same thing with the Holy Spirit. The more time we spend with Him, the more we start oozing out the fruits that are in Galatians 5.

I love the moments when I react totally different in a situation than I would have in the past. It helps me understand the power of boasting in my weakness and celebrating the goodness of God. It is also a great measuring point for me on how much I have grown spiritually. I love those moments and really desire to be like Him.

Imagine instead of being upset when someone does us wrong, we can feel the kindness of God filling our hearts to respond to them with love and understanding. Maybe in a moment when someone needs the truth, instead of delivering it really quick and bulldozing over their emotions, it's gentle and humble. In moments when we would have gone to a fast-food place and filled ourselves with junk, alcohol to feel better, or cigarettes to get over how we felt, we experience moments of self-control leading us to the Father's heart.

I love the triumphant moments of experiencing such a deep level of joy that negative thoughts can't even come near my thought process. What about experiencing God's peace that surpasses all understanding through heartache, chaos, or a loss? What about being faithful to protect your time in prayer when you could have replaced that time with social media, TV, a good book you're reading, or some other distraction? The more time we behold and engage the Holy Spirit, the more we fill ourselves up to respond to situations with maturity rather than react in our flesh.

PRAYING IN THE SPIRIT

When you are led by the Spirit and you read the word, you will discover all you need to know about Him. There are volumes of revelation, wisdom and understanding that could be and have been written on Him. I would like to share why I believe it's important for us to be praying in tongues as part of this Holy Revolution.

When I got baptized in the Holy Spirit, I got a phrase that I kept hearing over and over again but was too afraid to say out loud. After the baptism, I was praying that my mind wouldn't get in the way of me receiving my prayer language. I am one of those people who desires it to be absolutely God and no counterfeit of any kind. Remember, I didn't grow up around the charismatic culture, so this was naturally uncomfortable for me and I was ready to fight the fake.

Every time there was an altar call I would walk up and ask for someone on the ministry team to pray for me to receive my heavenly prayer language. I didn't want to make up some gibberish and I wanted to know that it was Him. I was hungry for this language. People would say, "Just open your mouth and speak," and I could not do it. I would feel like I was making it all up. Please keep in mind, many people do receive their prayer language that way. It's just not how I did.

One day there was a massive storm rolling into Texas. There was a tornado warning, which means there was tornado activity where I was. Alarms were going off, the sky was green and yellow, and I was driving home as safely and quickly as possible. Hardly anyone was on the road because of this storm. My parents were praying for me as I headed to the house because of the weather surrounding us.

As I was driving on the highway, I thought I ran over a massive tree branch. It was so loud, but I didn't see one on the road. I am not overexaggerating when I say that it was a piece of hail the size of a grapefruit or cantaloupe. It began to fall all around me, and without hesitation my left hand went up in the air, right hand on the wheel, and I began praying in tongues. I was in such shock that my reaction was tongues that I began crying and laughing while I was praying in the spirit. Fear could have come in, but instead my prayer language came out of me. Would you believe me if I told you that there was not one dent on my car? It was one of the biggest hailstorms we had, but I had not one dent and not one more piece of hail hit my car while I was driving back to my parents' house, even though it was pouring down all around me.

My first experience praying in tongues was super-natural protection from something that could have been scary. It was so real for me that I knew this gift was important. My first time praying in tongues was absolutely marvelous and still to this day I am amazed by God's divine protection.

> *For if you have the ability to speak in tongues, you will be talking only to God, since people won't be able to understand you. You will be speaking by the power of the Spirit, but it will all be mysterious* (1 Corinthians 14:2 NLT).

Another reason why I believe it's important is because you will be talking directly to our heavenly Father when you are praying in tongues. No one else can understand you unless they have the gift of inter-pretation, which I think is so cool. When we pray in the spirit, we are praying by the power of the Spirit—yes, the power—the same one that raised Jesus from the dead. It is so refreshing to walk, drive, or sit in a place where we can let go of everything happening throughout the day and just pray in the spirit and commune with our heavenly Father directly.

> *A person who speaks in tongues is strengthened personally, but one who speaks a word of prophecy strengthens the entire church* (1 Corinthians 14:4 NLT).

Speaking in tongues is one of those secret weapons that will strengthen you in ways that only praying in the spirit can. I want to be as strong and healthy as I possibly can be, and if that means that I need to pray in a heavenly language in order to accomplish that, sign me up! This is an absolute priority. Also, I do love that praying in tongues strengthens each of us. It's like our own treasure from the Holy Spirit, and it helps us in so many areas of our life.

There are many times when I have no idea what to do and I will pray in the spirit. Praying in the spirit is like praying the perfect prayer when you don't have words to know what to pray. I have found myself praying randomly under my breath out loud, and I assume in those moments the Holy Spirit is needing me to pray for something. I may not know what it is, but I know that it is accomplishing its work.

> *Likewise the Spirit helps us in our weakness. For we do not know what to pray for as we ought, but the Spirit himself*

*intercedes for us with groanings too deep
for words* (Romans 8:26 ESV).

There will be many times when the enemy will try
to taunt us with our weakness or when we will not feel
adequate as others who have different gifts than us
if we don't stay prayed up in the Spirit. It is healthy
to recognize our weaknesses and recognize the battles ahead that we cannot win on our own. We have a
Friend who is praying the perfect prayers through us
in all of these situations and He will bring the victory.
So, friends, let's pray in the Spirit. Paul understood the
value of this gift and I encourage you to go read more
about it in First Corinthians 12–14.

In times of fasting it's really helpful when I get up
and walk around praying in tongues. In times of heaviness, I can pray in the spirit *until* I feel the shift of
breakthrough. There are times when I pray in tongues
and a random answer I needed days before comes into
my mind and the blueprint just flows right now. This
gift is full of fun surprises. Most often I feel like I could
run a spiritual marathon after praying in the spirit,
and other times it has led me to weeping. I love this
gift and I do believe it is a powerful weapon to have in
your belt as we approach the days ahead together.

PRAYER FOR HOLINESS

*Holy Spirit, I love You. I invite You to come
fill every part of me. Would You be my best*

friend? Would You reveal heaven's secrets to me? I want to walk with You in the day and I want to dream with You in the night. Thank You for all of our adventures we have together. I am honored to get to know You more. Amen.

Chapter 5

THE WINNING TEAM

Warriors never pray for comfort, they pray to do the will of their Father.

—BRISKILLA ZANANIRI

If we want to become unshakable and joyful no matter what comes our way then we need to know how to pray. Prayer, especially intercession, is always being on the winning team and never losing. Having a powerful prayer life is having heaven's secret service surround you and protect you every moment of every day. Prayer is how you discover the immaculate nuances of our heavenly Father and it empowers you to walk in His ways. He reveals secret blueprints in prayer and gives us warning so that we can be prepared. When we understand how to pray, we learn how to stand until we see God do exactly what He said He was going to do.

The place of prayer is the core of the Holy Revolution. It will be the secret weapon of victory we carry into every single battle, no matter how big or small. Anytime a revival came it's been measured that each one stopped when prayer stopped. Prayer is the momentum that keeps hearts alive and burning with heaven on earth. We cannot let this weapon sit on the shelf and collect dust or our hearts will grow sick, and we have too much work to do together for that to happen. Prayer also waters our hearts with the Spirit of God.

I have found forgiveness, healing, mercy, love, thankfulness, His faithfulness, and more in this place. I have found direction, correction, compassion, and hope in this place. Most importantly, I have found Him. Faith has been built in the places of prayer as my prayers became the prayers of heaven rather than my own personal opinions. Jesus Himself chose to go sit at the right hand of the Father to pray for each of us, and then He told us that we are seated in heavenly places with Him.

> *And God raised us up with Christ and seated us with him in the heavenly realms in Christ Jesus* (Ephesians 2:6 NIV).

My desire and my goal is to be led by the Holy Spirit in prayer so that I can hear what Jesus is praying as the great intercessor of heaven and come into agreement with that on earth, rather than human wisdom.

Many of us have not really been taught how to pray yet. We have just been told to. Jesus only said what He heard the Father say and did what He saw our Father do. This means His prayer life and ability to hear the Lord was in tune to perfect pitch. He lived this way to show us that we are called to do the same.

THE MOST POWERFUL WEAPON

I was running from the cops one night. I had no idea why they were chasing after me. Yes, this is a dream I had. I was not afraid, but I was aware that I either knew something that they needed or was carrying something I didn't know I was carrying. So I ran, looking for my father. When I found him I told him what was happening; he looked me in the eyes and said, "Jamie, it's time for you to know what your most powerful weapon on earth is." In my utmost mature fashion I literally yelled, *"Fire."* I wish I could insert a laughing face right here. He turned as a helmet began to come from the sky. He looked at me and began to place it on my head and said, "No, your most power- ful weapon on earth is prayer." Y'all, I woke up and nearly threw my Bible. This was so powerful, real, and tangible to me that I was deeply honored that I knew something so special.

The best part about all of this is that prayer is relationship with God. I cannot believe that the rela- tionship I have with God is my most powerful weapon on earth. It's not some fireball I muster up and throw at the enemy like we see in movies. It's not some high kick to satan's face—it's time with my Father. Selah.

THE LORD'S PRAYER

> *Our Father in heaven, hallowed be your name, your kingdom come, your will be done, on earth as it is in heaven. Give us today our daily bread. And forgive us our debts, as we also have forgiven our debtors. And lead us not into temptation, but deliver us from the evil one* (Matthew 6:9-13 NIV).

Jesus shows us how to pray right here when we don't know how to pray. He starts off by acknowledging the holiness of our God. He asks God for His will to be made complete on earth rather than His own personal desires. He then asks God for everything He needs for today. One of my favorite parts is when He shows us the power of repentance and forgiveness. Lord, forgive me for what I have done wrong, and I forgive those who have wronged me. Lord, keep me from the temptations of this world and deliver me from the enemy.

> *If you abide in me, and my words abide in you, ask whatever you wish, and it will be done for you* (John 15:7 ESV).

The more time we spend in the word and in prayer, the more we come to know the heart of our Father.

I want to share some scriptures with you that have taught me that knowing Him makes my prayers more effective.

> *When you ask, you do not receive, because you ask with wrong motives, that you may spend what you get on your pleasures* (James 4:3 NIV).

I reached a time when I had to be really honest with myself. I was tired of prayer and the secret place was all about me, my dreams, and how I wanted them to come true. It became exhausting talking about me, me, me all the time. I began to pray for others out loud, and I began to listen to Him and what He wanted to do more, and it changed my prayer life. Now, I am at a point where the dreams I used to have in the natural feel completely empty because they did not have Him in them. All I want is to live each moment of every day with Him.

There can actually be dreams within us that could keep us from Him. We could be asking Him, in good spirit, for gifts, for promotions, for that guy or girl to like us, for someone to change, for a new house, a new car, or for that one big break for our dreams to come to pass. It can be well meaning, but it can also be something that could become an idol if He answered that prayer. In fact, it might be an idol already or simply something He doesn't have for you. His rejection is your protection. The more we spend time with Him, the more we discover what His dreams for us are. When He becomes your dream, He makes the other dreams look small. So how are you praying when no one is around? It's a healthy question to ask yourself.

> *You draw near to those who call out to you, listening closely, especially when their hearts are true. Every one of your godly lovers receives even more than what they ask for. For you hear what their hearts really long for and you bring them your saving strength* (Psalm 145:18-19 TPT).

Psalm 145 in *The Passion Translation* brings tears to my eyes. A heart that is holy and on fire for Jesus cannot help but desire what God created them to desire. A life that has been transformed by Jesus can no longer desire the things that led them down a path of destruction. It's called the narrow path, and so few find it because so few are willing to give up everything to remain on this path. To the world, these holy ones are absolutely crazy. Well, call me crazy! God leans down, listens, and out-dreams every single one of His holy and pure-hearted vessels. I ask again, have you found this in Him yet? If not, do you want to live a life of prayer where you are more than satisfied because you know He will do what He said He is going to do?

THE SECRET PLACE

But when you pray, go into your room and shut the door and pray to your Father who is in secret. And your Father who sees in secret will reward you (Matthew 6:6 ESV).

Praying with others is very powerful. But there is something unbelievably special that happens when you take time away from the crowds, like Jesus did, to abide with just you and the Father. There are moments that happen here that only you and heaven will know about. There are secrets that God wants to share with you on how to pray for others and how to pray for situations, and it will require you to protect this place with God. You also get to watch amazing situations completely change in people's lives, who will never know you were praying for them, and it is fuel to your prayer life. We get to celebrate the victories that we got to be part of in prayer.

I remember one of my leaders asked me if I thought the public prayer room was any different from the secret place. I said, "Absolutely." He then began to tell me that he did not think they were any different. For him, he didn't have time because of kids and family, which I often heard from parents when I was a children's pastor, and the prayer room was his secret place with God. I remember feeling grieved. I didn't understand why he felt they were the same. Nothing to argue about—I kept it in my heart.

We will always make time for what we value. We will always make a way. Parents, you can find time while you are making dinner or the kids are napping, by waking up a tad earlier or going to bed a little later, when driving in the car or going to work out. This is not to guilt trip anyone. This is to encourage you to have your time of prayer as the Holy Spirit will show you how you can do this alone with God each day.

When you are married, there are conversations that are deep and intimate and things that a husband and wife do that are deep and intimate that you would never share with anyone else. I would say that's the equivalent to the secret place with God. There is something that happens uniquely for you and God that can only be found when you are alone with Him. I would protect this place and guard it with everything you have. I don't know if that man still feels that way about the secret place and the public prayer room, but I did not allow that to take me away from that special place I have with God. You must remember, not everyone in your journey will have the same convictions you do. Just because they are older and not on the same page does not give us permission to forgo the things we feel the Holy Spirit is leading us into.

LISTENING

Prayer is having a conversation with Him, and there are creative and unique ways to do this. It's a relationship where you're not just speaking but also listening. It's an amount of time you carve out to specifically speak and connect with Jesus. When you grab coffee with a friend, you don't talk the whole time or you would never get to know them. You ask them questions and you listen to what is going on in their lives, how they are doing, and what they are planning on doing. It is the same with God. We grow this partnership and friendship with Him to understand what He wants to do, and it changes everything.

In November of 2020 I was at a prayer rally that my father-in-love was hosting in D.C. There were hundreds of baby boomers who arrived early that morning, and it was cold and pouring down rain. My gut response was, "This is the Lord" and then also, "Wow, these warriors are standing out here because they believe in why we are gathered." My flesh response was, "Let's command this rain to stop so they don't have to be miserable out here." My spiritual mom got up on stage to come pray with us and said, "Rain often represents a curse breaking in the land. Warriors never pray for comfort; they pray to do the will of the Father." Wow. Instead of telling the rain to go away, we thanked Him for it.

I learned the power of really tuning into the Lord in situations like this instead of operating in my flesh.

Even taking a moment to ask Him, "Lord, what are You saying about the rain?" He told us this date. He knew we were coming, and listening to Him was part of prayer in this moment and then taking the time to lead the group in prayer for what He wanted to do.

The success of the Holy Revolution will come when we learn the value of listening to God and responding in action if required. His voice is the victory in every blueprint for every battle.

I love what Patricia King said one time: "It isn't a discipline to read the word and spend time with God; it's a privilege." When we start viewing our daily connection points with God as a privilege, it changes everything. I think of famous people and how amazing it would be if someone you admired wanted to spend time with you for a day. You would take it. God Himself desires to spend time with us and we have full access to Him 24/7, 365 days a year. He is the one who created everything good. He is always available to those who will seek Him.

GATHER THE PEOPLE TO PRAY

I loved being part of Upper Room Dallas in the beginning days. Now it's a massive church and prayer room, and I have never seen the heart of this house change. They have been faithful to do only what the Father has led them to do. I grew up very quickly there spiritually. We watched as a city started to gather and a family began to form around the place of prayer throughout each week. Sunday services were great, but what happened in the prayer room was even better.

> *Again I say to you, if two of you agree on earth about anything they ask, it will be done for them by my Father in heaven* (Matthew 18:19 ESV).

Gathering with other brothers and sisters and coming into agreement with the heart and will of our Father is very important and very powerful. From this place each uniquely gifted person comes forward and prays as a beautiful picture is painted. This is where families, churches, businesses, school districts, cities, states, and nations will be transformed and where we will be transformed in the very presence of God through prayer.

I have seen numerous men and women, including myself, be totally transformed by the presence of God as we gathered together to pray. People who struggled with homosexuality would months later be transformed by the love, the truth, the word, and the presence of our heavenly Father. Miraculous healing would take place in people's hearts, bodies, and minds. Hate would be extracted from people's hearts and hope would fill them. Barren women would carry healthy, full-term babies, and the injured would be made whole. You never really knew what was going to happen in the prayer room, but you knew the Holy

Spirit would show up and take everyone to Jesus. Gathering people to pray is very important.

If you are called to rally millions of people to pray to our faithful Father—first, be faithful when no one is looking, and be faithful with what the Holy Spirit leads you to build with Him here. Gather families in your home and start praying together. Watch what God does as you continue to be His faithful one.

WALKING HOUSE OF PRAYER

I had a dream in which Heidi Baker (symbolically representing Jesus) came to me and confirmed three things in my life. One was my husband, two was the city we are called to, and three was that I was called to establish the house of prayer everywhere I go because I am a house of prayer. That was such a serious eye-opener. We are called to gather and pray. We are called to be walking houses of prayer. We are called to commune with our heavenly Father and others everywhere we go. She didn't tell me I was going to be a television show host, author, or speaker. No, she told me I am a house of prayer.

When we each gave our lives to Jesus, it changed everything. When we each got baptized in the Holy Spirit, we became a dwelling place for the Lord to come and rest within us. This is why I believe it is so important for us to keep every gate closed to sin and darkness so that the Lord would find a pure house to dwell in. So that when He speaks to us, we can hear

Him without any junk to filter it through. As walking houses of prayer, there are things God is going to reveal to us because we are positioned to hear Him.

> *This is what we speak, not in words taught us by human wisdom but in words taught by the Spirit, explaining spiritual realities with Spirit-taught words* (1 Corinthians 2:13 NIV).

As walking houses of prayer and dwelling places of the Lord, we will be taught things that can only be taught by the Holy Spirit. We can walk into a store, school, or event and pray what He desires us to pray. I often drive by cars and feel prompted to pray for them, so I do. When we recognize we are a walking house of prayer, our eyes are opened everywhere we go to know how to pray and what to pray. Prayer changes everything. Where prayer is, God is. Therefore, we are walking around with God when we access a life of prayer.

INTERCESSION

Oftentimes, we think intercessors are these old women sitting in a closet praying for other people. While that might be true in many cases, I find it hard to believe that anyone in the Holy Revolution would not experience intercession at some point or another. When God gives you a burden in His heart for something, you weep, you pray, you find out His solution, and you pray it through until you see it. Jesus Himself is an intercessor at the right hand of the Father in heaven right now. This type of prayer is coming into agreement with what God has said in His word and is saying right now and not moving from that place until it happens.

The righteous will never be uprooted, but the wicked will not remain in the land (Proverbs 10:30 NIV).

The more you stand and agree with God, the stronger it will make you in seasons of shaking in your family, your state, or your nation. When you see the faithfulness of God in some of the craziest situations, you know that He will never lose a battle that is meant to be won by Him. I have had the sheer joy of watching God turn the hardest heart back to Him, restore broken families, bring life into the womb of one who was barren, extract the wicked from places and make sure the righteous remain, and more. We serve a God of strategy, and we get to come to the table with Him to see the plans and make sure they happen.

I believe intercessors are some of the most prophetic men and women on earth. They take what they hear from the Father and they establish it on earth. Sometimes they do it alone, and other times they gather others to agree and pray. They are not looking for a place to be seen because they know their place in heaven.

God gives intercessors assignments for different spheres of influence and situations. One of my favorite parts of being an intercessor is that it's like being a secret agent for heaven and getting to celebrate and pray for people who have no idea you're one of the ones praying. Then you get to watch God be victorious in those situations and people's lives. Intercessors are like football players playing offense and they can't lose. The quarterback, Jesus, throws them the ball from heaven and they run and make the touchdown. Sometimes they get tackled, but they get right back up, and when they do they find that God wins every time. It does require our perseverance to see it through.

How will you know if you're supposed to intercede for someone or something? First of all, something will come to your mind that you cannot shake. It could be a frustration or a heavy burden—a burden that's holy and desires to see people set free and protected. Sometimes I am so gripped with weeping, I know there is something for me to seek the Lord on. Second, you can just ask Him if you're to carry this through in prayer. He will always lead you and guide you here.

PRAYING FOR LEADERS

I urge, then, first of all, that petitions, prayers, intercession and thanksgiving be made for all people—for kings and all those in authority, that we may live peaceful and quiet lives in all godliness and holiness. This is good, and pleases God our Savior, who wants all people to be saved and to come to a knowledge of the truth (1 Timothy 2:1-4 NIV).

Prayer is not always about you. I remember literally being annoyed and exhausted in a season of my early 20s when I realized my prayer time was about me and not about the Father's desires. You can tell when someone is praying for someone or for a situation. They don't slander or speak evil about them. They aren't in denial if someone or something is evil, but they have hope for their lives in Christ Jesus. It is never too late for anyone to know God and to turn their heart to Him. We have the honor of praying and blessing our enemies. We have the honor of praying for those in leadership who are doing well and who really need to live a life that's led by the Holy Spirit. Every prayer we pray is powerful, and in James 5:16 it says that "The prayer of a righteous person is powerful and effective" (NIV).

Oftentimes, it may be the person who bothers us the most that we are called to pray for. If you have unkind or malicious thoughts toward someone, I want to encourage you to ask God for His heart for them and to begin to pray for them. It will soften your heart and His kindness will bring us to repentance each time. Then we have the authority to serve them well and speak into their lives, if He calls us to. Prayer changes the way we see others from a worldly view to a heavenly one.

PRAYER

Our Father in heaven, holy is Your name; Your kingdom come, Your will be done on earth as it is in heaven. Thank You for providing everything I need today. Forgive me for all wrong I have done, as I also forgive those who have wronged me. And lead me away from temptation and keep me from the enemy's hands. Amen.

Chapter 6

THE *SWORD* OF GOD

*Opinion is the lowest form of human
knowledge.*

—TIM SPIRES

Many men and women have watered down scripture and the gospel to help others feel more comfortable or to justify their own personal lifestyle. It's a dangerous road, and in order to keep our way pure we must guard it with God's written word. We will never find freedom in the world's way of doing things. The true and uncompromising message of the gospel is what sets bound men and women free. When we read the word of God, we discover God Himself. The more I learn, the more I realize I have so much more to learn. It's very humbling, and His word becomes an adventure of discovering Him.

> *How can a young man keep his way
> pure? By guarding it according to your
> word* (Psalm 119:9 ESV).

We will never find freedom by agreeing with sin or evil in small doses here or there. In John 17:17 it says, "Sanctify them in the truth; your word is truth" (ESV), and we all know that the truth is what sets us free. So many of us are looking for freedom, and it is found in the man Jesus and He is one page flip away in our Bibles from being discovered even more.

THE WRITTEN *SWORD* OF GOD

For the word of God is living and active, sharper than any two-edged sword, piercing to the division of soul and of spirit, of joints and of marrow, and discerning the thoughts and intentions of the heart (Hebrews 4:12 ESV).

You can't spell *sword* without the *word!* This sword will help you win battles that can only be won by the wisdom of God. The sword referred to here in this scripture is a scalpel. A tool that is extremely sharp and does the intricately detailed work to get inside a human body. The word of God helps us discern precisely what should be within and what should remain apart from us.

The word of God is one of the most romantic books I have ever read and the most informative about love itself. There is a man who sat with prostitutes, killers, slanderers, the brokenhearted, the castaways, the weak, the mistreated, and sick and called them beloved. He literally spent time with people most of us would walk on by, and He showed them so much love. He had no judgment or criticism to extend because His whole being was love. Only He can do what He has done for you and me in our lives. This love and this romance is interwoven throughout every parable, character, and chapter of the Bible.

It is perfectly normal to have moments when you don't "feel like" reading your Bible. It's what you do in those moments that changes the game. We read it anyway and we find freedom that helps us discern the thoughts and intentions of our own hearts. Also, Jesus said that He would send His helper to help us.

If you need desire to be awakened for you to read the word, just ask for it. Remember we were given free will. If you're wanting to supernaturally learn how to play the piano but you're not taking lessons or sitting in front of the piano trying, you'll never know if He answered your prayers or not. So ask for the desire, but then open the book and read it. If you need hunger in your gut to spend time with God and an understanding of the scriptures when you read it, just ask Him for it before you start reading and then read and you will find it.

I used to have a difficult time, feeling like I could never remember or understand what I was reading, until I fell in love with Jesus. Now, I am so mesmerized by His goodness that I can't wait to read about Him each day. This is my prayer for you and for me—that we would long to read the word and understand it in our hearts. That we would take the time to spend each day in His word to understand and grow in Him.

> *Every Scripture has been written by the Holy Spirit, the breath of God. It will empower you by its instruction and correction, giving you the strength to take the right direction and lead you deeper into the path of godliness* (2 Timothy 3:16 TPT).

Y'all, the word was written for us back in the day because God knew we would need leadership, empowerment, and strength today. When I read it, there are moments when it leads me to repentance. There are moments when it highlights the way for me to keep walking. There are moments when I feel a paralysis of fear and it wakes me up to realize that this little life of mine is detrimental to heaven on earth.

I read about the great, great men and women of faith in Moses, Esther, Daniel, Joshua, Caleb, Paul, James, and more. They have transformed my life to see that no matter the cost, following the word, because He is the word, is supreme and worth everything—even my own life. They were faced with difficulties time and time again. Many of them freaked out, and He allowed us to see it. When it came time to face the darkness with the light-bearing word of God, they did it and we get to as well. We are eternal beings and we must recognize that our own lives are just a fragment of what we really get to spend with Him forever.

Blessed rather are those who hear the word of God and obey it (Luke 11:28 NIV).

Will we comfort culture when she is crying out for acceptance through sin or will we point her to her true identity? The word of God is very clear on what a godly life is and what it is not. We cannot discover these truths without fueling our body with them. There is a tug-of-war with culture and the word in many people's lives.

When Jesus ended His 40-day fast in the desert, satan came to Him. He tempted Jesus with "the word" but twisted it, and Jesus knew better. Do you know how many times throughout our lives the word gets twisted? Even by preachers today. We have the "prosperity gospel" all about money and what you can have while you're on earth, and really all those things are things that wither away. Those pastors are embracing greed and material items rather than seeking first the kingdom of heaven. We have the "grace" gospel, which many young men and women have been led to, where it's okay if you sin because He will cover it when really His grace empowers us to live holy and not sin.

Can I hear the people yell amen from the back of the room, please? We gotta be careful out there on those streets today, y'all. We need this word inside us so when satan comes at us with his handsome look and charm we feel detest toward the invitation and joyfully say, "Not today, satan." Reading the word gives us courage to obey the word. What we let in comes out, and I will keep saying that over and over again in this book. I have been set free from so much darkness because I am fueling my body with the word of God. It's the best steak you could ever eat, and this Texan woman loves her some steak. Thank You, Jesus!

THE ABSOLUTE BASELINE

> *For our struggle is not against flesh and blood, but against the rulers, against the authorities, against the powers of this dark world and against the spiritual forces of evil in the heavenly realms* (Ephesians 6:12 NIV).

In a world filled with men and women who love to debate one another rather than the ideas themselves, we must understand what our baseline really is. I love what my husband told me once: "As believers, we play by a different set of rules." We do not play by the rules of this world where people argue with one another until the winner comes out on top. We stand firmly rooted in the word of God for all of eternity. After all, there is a spiritual battle and we will fight according to whatever spirit we are allowing to lead us.

My dad, Tim, and I have amazing conversations about the word of God. He is a very anointed teacher and I learn so much from him every time we have a conversation. He shared with me once, "Opinion is the lowest form of human knowledge. When we are arguing about matters of opinion, there is no baseline for truth. Our opinion should be based on something other than our feelings. The word of God gives us a baseline from which to form our beliefs and opinions. If our discussions can be around the word of God rather than our opinions, then we have a good baseline for discussion." We do see a lot of young men and women who are being led by their emotions and their opinions. This is dangerous because we are held accountable for every idle word as mentioned in Matthew 12:36.

Preach the word; be prepared in season and out of season; correct, rebuke and encourage—with great patience and careful instruction (2 Timothy 4:2 NIV).

It's important when someone asks us cultural questions that we are able to refer them to the word of God rather than our own opinion, because our opinion carries no weight. I know many who have memorized the word yet bear no fruit because they have no relationship with Jesus. They quote it yet live in deep sin. If we don't have the relationship with Jesus to back up the written words, it can cause more damage than good when sharing the gospel. We must be patient and gentle with people when we preach. If they do not see the character of Christ in us when we are pointing them to Him or scriptures, they will not want Him. Jesus is the most incredible human who has ever walked planet earth, and when we understand how to draw people to Him He is undeniably desirable.

THE TEACHER

So Jesus said to the Jews who had believed him, "If you abide in my word, you are truly my disciples, and you will know the truth, and the truth will set you free" (John 8:31-32 ESV).

The greatest teacher on planet earth is Jesus. When we read the words He spoke to us throughout the gospels, we see that His words are always applicable to today. Still, He leads us to the Father. Each time we read the scriptures, a new revelation can come from it that applies to situations we are in or that are to come. He, in His kindness, gave us a book filled with answers and the ability to approach Him boldly and hear directly from Him.

We are living in a world that is longing for the truth. We are called to abide in His word, and that will lead us to the truth we are looking for. It is supernatural to remember how dark my world was. To many others, I was a pure-hearted vessel. When I see where He has brought me from to now, the truth alone set me free and has put a fire in me that can never go out. I did not even know I was in darkness because of the pride and self-inflicted hate toward myself that seeped into my heart. When we fill ourselves with His word, it reveals the truth, gives space for us to repent, and sets us free. Agreeing with His word and doing it brings blessing.

THE SPOKEN WORD

When the Spirit of truth comes, he will guide you into all the truth, for he will not speak on his own authority, but whatever he hears he will speak, and he will declare to you the things that are to come (John 16:13 ESV).

I love the prophetic gift. The first time I ever received a prophetic word I was absolutely stunned. I was also sweating and scared out of my mind. I knew that no one could have known anything that they were sharing with me unless they heard the Lord or were walking closely with me. I felt seen and known by God. It absolutely changed my life and made me realize the supernatural was still relevant today. That is the beauty of His voice. It helps us feel seen and known by Him. His voice draws us closer to Him. There are things that God wants to share with us through His Holy Spirit. It could be while we are reading the word or it could be in whatever way He has gifted us to hear Him.

My sheep hear my voice, and I know them, and they follow me (John 10:27 ESV).

The Lord is our shepherd and we are His sheep. He gave us the free will to follow Him and listen to what He has to say today. His voice is not just for us, but it's also meant to bless everyone around us when we hear Him. I love hearing what God has to say about other people. Most of the time, I am able to share it with them and it helps encourage them in what they have been praying about. Sometimes, God shares things with me about people so I can intercede for them.

His voice is always encouraging and protecting us on the pathway to eternal life with Him. I love hearing people tell me how accurate a word is that I shared with them or how life-changing it was for them. Most of the time I don't remember the word, but every time someone gives me positive feedback I am in awe of how real God is. I never want to lose that wonder and awe of God. I could never know these amazing things for others if I didn't hear His voice. Therefore, I turn to Him and I thank Him when encouraging feedback comes in. The gift does not make me great. I do not make myself great. It is my God who is great within me.

When I was the children's pastor at Upper Room in Dallas, the one thing I knew children needed to know early on was how to hear the voice of God. When you seek Jesus and His voice, you get Jesus and His voice. These children were learning the word and they were learning how they hear His voice. We would practice soaking, which is turning on music and asking God a question. This taught them to listen to Him and spend time with Him. We would also practice hearing His voice during times of prophecy over adults, volunteers, or other kids. This gave them courage and began to normalize a life in which they could hear God all throughout the day no matter where they are.

Follow the way of love and eagerly desire gifts of the Spirit, especially prophecy (1 Corinthians 14:1 NIV).

I want to encourage you to practice listening to His voice all throughout the day. If you need to get together with friends or sign up for a prophecy class in your city or online, do it. The spoken word of God is revealed by the Holy Spirit, and we all have the ability to do this. God is taking men and women into every sphere of influence to prophesy. We have government leaders, education boards, cities, businesses, church leadership, moms, dads, military units, creatives, builders, students, and more who need to be encouraged and strengthened by the voice of God. You could be the one He sends to encourage them and help the plans of heaven be implemented on earth. Sometimes you may be sent in a sneaky, undercover way and what you share sounds like a brilliant plan and idea, but secretly it is from God.

I had the honor of hearing a model preach who lives in California. She has so much favor in modeling, and when she goes to runway shows or photo shoots she prays for healing and prophesies over the men and women backstage. They began to call her the prophet. She never gave herself that title; they did. They are so hungry for truth and encouragement that she has immense favor in the background of this sphere of influence. She has been seated in boardrooms with huge influencers to prophesy the word of God. Practice this gift. One day, you could be helping unbelievers who are extremely talented and gifted know the voice of God and choose to give their everything to Jesus.

At our wedding, we had a few men and women speak who shared valuable insight and prophetic words into our marriage. They were words that were extremely important for us as an anchor in what God has called us to. One of them was wisdom and the importance of us carrying wisdom everywhere Lance and I go. Do you know that because someone shared these words, I took that spoken word over our marriage and dove straight into the word of God to learn more about it? Y'all, I am so grateful for the book of Proverbs and for First Corinthians 2. When I read about the spirit of wisdom, I fall in love with her more and more. She is so flipping cool. We get to discover these tools and the spoken word of God through the written word of God too. It is so imperative that we fill our hearts with this written love and take seriously the prophetic words that are spoken over our lives.

HONORING THE WORD OF THE PROPHET

The one who receives a prophet because he is a prophet will receive a prophet's reward, and the one who receives a righteous person because he is a righteous person will receive a righteous person's reward (Matthew 10:41 ESV).

When you read the Old Testament, it is filled with scriptures about how kings would seek the wisdom of true prophets or prophets would approach kings with the word of the Lord. They were pivotal in times when they chose to hear the word of the Lord and when they didn't. How many times did it take for Pharaoh to hear the word of the Lord from Moses? At least ten times. People suffered because of his pride, and then finally he let the Lord's people go. Moses and Aaron kept being faithful to come back and deliver the word because they heard the voice of God and obeyed it.

Remember too that those who receive a righteous person will receive a righteous person's reward. The righteous reward is a life lived with Jesus on earth and for eternity. There will be people who are offended because of the holiness within you. Truth can be very offensive to many people because it would require them being "wrong" or giving up their comforts or desires in order to come into agreement with the way you live. Has this not happened to each of us? Now, we can meet people with grace, humility, and love because we have been met by God in this way.

I always want my heart to be positioned to see what God is doing and come into agreement with Him. If Noah were alive today and building a giant ark in the middle of the desert, I would want to be on that ark with him when the rain came. I wouldn't want to be scoffing at him on the sidelines. It is very important for us to weigh each word before the Lord. I would imagine that the broad path will be speaking one thing and the narrow will be speaking another as we move forward. The narrow path requires a knowing of His word, both spoken and written. This will differentiate the Holy Revolution from the mainstream Christians. It's not "us versus them." It will be humility, love, and obedience to Him and Him alone that differentiates the two.

Continue to bless those who do not accept your words and pray for them. Continue to live righteous and holy as He is holy, because you never know how many seeds you are planting in the hearts of those who are watching or who are walking close to you. Jesus was not accepted even by the religious leaders of His day. They were too bound by the law to see from the lens of heaven. Prophetic words and righteousness do not always look to people the way they think they should. Those who accept the prophet and the righteous person will be blessed. We don't have to fight for people to hear us, recognize us, or honor us. The Lord accepts us and loves us, and that should be more than enough to keep being faithful to our master.

PRAYER

Lord, I thank You for Your written and spoken word. I ask, Holy Spirit, for You to reveal to me the heart of our Father when I read the word. Would You help me discover You while I read and pray? I love You and I thank You for helping me grow. Amen.

Chapter 7

FUNDAMENTALS FIRST

The revolution we are part of is one that revolves solely around the man Jesus. With Him as our core and focus, everything falls perfectly into place. I loved hearing Patricia King share one time, "It isn't God first, family second, and job third. It's God first." I am not hating on anyone who says that three-step priority list. When Jesus is our center, everything truly flows from that place as He reveals what we need to know and how much time to put in it.

There are things revealed to us in the word that draw us closer to Him and remind us of the value of Him being our center. It's not by a legalistic set of rules that we do this but because of our deep love and affection for Him. In fact, Jesus Himself walked in these wonderful practices. I have found that the following tools have helped me grow and mature spiritually to recognize the God of the impossible is always faithful and really who He says He is. I pray that as you read this it spurs you on to keep watering your heart with the Spirit and feeding it with the word. These spiritual principles were created for us to commune with our heavenly Jesus as we journey through this Holy Revolution in great discipline.

THANKSGIVING

Do not be anxious about anything, but in everything by prayer and supplication with thanksgiving let your requests be made known to God (Philippians 4:6 ESV).

No matter what circumstance we are in, we are called to make our requests for that hour known through thanksgiving. I always begin my prayers this way to the Father. I stop and stand before Him and begin to thank God for who He is and what He has done. As I do this, it fills me with faith and reminds me that He is faithful to keep being, you guessed it, faithful. I love submitting my emotions, thoughts, and feelings to the place of thanksgiving in agreement with everything He has done. It also tends to completely change what I thought I would be praying for because I realize that the situation is a lot more peaceful with Him as the victor.

We are moving into a time on earth when thanksgiving will be a huge key to winning the battles. There will be many things that look very impossible, that look evil and dark as they try to continue to take over places and spaces, but thanksgiving will remind us of His great power and plans. It will position our hearts from complaining and doubt to expectancy and faith.

When I worked at Upper Room in Dallas, we were meeting above a veterinary clinic. We had grown to be so big that the fire marshal kept coming in and shutting us down. He would give us new codes that we would follow or news of what else we needed to do in order to stay open. It got to the point in staff meetings that when bad news would come, we would stand up, some on our chairs, cheering, laughing, and thanking God because we knew He had the answer for us to keep this house of prayer open and keep serving Him. Instead of feeling anxious about what to do and afraid of closing down, we presented our requests to the Lord with thanksgiving and it gave us joy in the journey that was difficult.

> *Rejoice always, pray without ceasing, give thanks in all circumstances; for this is the will of God in Christ Jesus for you* (1 Thessalonians 5:16-18 ESV).

We could not see the answers, nor did we know what would happen during this time, but I remember we would thank God before we had the answer. It is the will of Jesus in our lives to rejoice always, to pray without ceasing, and give thanks in every circumstance! If this is His will for us, how much more precious should this be in our daily lives? Have you ever had news that just made you feel helpless and every option looked impossible? His will for us is to be thankful and rejoice in Him even during these moments. When our trust is in Him alone, He is easy to thank. He carries the solution.

Even if you don't know how the victory will come, I want to encourage you to say, "Thank You, Jesus, for coming in as our victor in this situation. You are good and You are faithful. I cannot wait to see what You do. I thank You for revealing the plans You have and helping me serve You in this journey." Prayers like this will make the journey much more beautiful and allow you to feel Him so near in these moments. It also helps us remain humble, understanding that we cannot live without Him. We are dependent on Him in each situation.

> *Enter his gates with thanksgiving and his courts with praise; give thanks to him and praise his name* (Psalm 100:4 NIV).

I love reading Psalm 100 because when we begin to thank Him He shows up in a moment because we have entered His gates. We have stepped into His presence, and in that place transformation happens. When you are thanking someone, you thank them to their face, not to someone else. You can sing someone's praises behind their back when they are not around. However, thanksgiving is very personal in nature. We come to our Father directly, face to face to say, "Thank You, Father. I agree with who You are."

Dr. Caroline Leaf has changed my life with her studies of the brain. She is a Christian neurologist, and one of her posts on Instagram in November of 2020 shared five ways gratitude helps us. One of them was a "free anti-depressant." When we express gratitude and receive the same, our brain releases dopamine and serotonin, the two crucial neurotransmitters responsible for our emotions, and they make us feel good. "They enhance our mood immediately making us feel happy from the inside."

This is the good news, ladies and gentlemen. Get that thanksgiving and gratitude out of those lips with those words. It'll be a game-changer from the inside out and change the atmosphere for you. I have had moments when I felt poopy and the last thing I wanted to do was give thanks. The moment I did, with my words, it changed my perspective and released the heaviness and brought peace and joy.

WORSHIP

Worship is a mighty weapon. It's a moment in times of difficulty and impossibility when we walk toward the battle with the song of the Lord declaring who our Victor is. In Second Chronicles 20, we see King Jehoshaphat was informed that armies were coming to wage war against them. He called all of Judah to a fast as they sought the Lord for guidance. Jehoshaphat stood up before all of the people and began to declare the goodness of God. He reminded the Lord of the inheritance that He gave them and that their army was not suitable to overcome those who were rising up against them. At the end the king said in verse 12, "We do not know what to do, but our eyes are on you" (NIV). I love this passage. It even goes on to say that "All the men of Judah, with their wives and children and little ones, stood there before the Lord" (2 Chron. 20:13 NIV). Families came together to seek the Lord in times of trouble in the nation. This is so powerful.

A prophet named Jahaziel came forth to reveal the battle was indeed the Lord's and they were not to be afraid. Then the nation fell before the Lord in worship. The king encouraged them to have faith in the Lord and have faith in the word from the prophet, then they would be successful. Faith is an important part of worship. Even when we cannot see it and it doesn't make sense, will we agree with who God is?

> *After consulting the people, Jehoshaphat appointed men to sing to the Lord and to praise him for the splendor of his holiness as they went out at the head of the army saying: "Give thanks to the Lord, for his love endures forever"* (2 Chronicles 20:21 NIV).

I love that the worshipers went out before the army to declare their victory and who their trust was in! Not only did they believe in God and win the battle, but on the fourth day they assembled together to worship the Lord and give Him thanks. Then as they entered Jerusalem, they worshiped the Lord again! When the news had spread among the kingdoms what had happened, the fear of the Lord came upon them and their nation was at rest. Worship is unbelievably powerful and reminds us of who God is and that He will do what He said He is going to do. Wow!

We have many battles ahead of us, and it's important for us to know the word of the Lord as we go forth declaring who He is. Fasting, worship, and prayer quiets all that's around us for the strategies of God to be heard and for the crowd to be silenced in chaos. The prophets are still speaking today, and it could even be you to whom He is speaking to deliver the word of victory. He shows up and shows off in our weakness to show that He is real and that He is good. We must protect our time in worship on the front line of battle.

Worship is one of the most powerful and immaculate things we get to do while we are here on earth, and I would call it supernatural. We will be doing this for all of eternity, yet we get to do it in the midst of some of the darkest days on earth. Our lives are worship to Him, and there is no better picture than that of Revelation 4.

> *The twenty-four elders fall down before him who sits on the throne and worship him who lives for ever and ever. They lay*

their crowns before the throne and say: "You are worthy, our Lord and God, to receive glory and honor and power, for you created all things, and by your will they were created and have their being" (Revelation 4:10-11 NIV).

Day and night there are elders gathered around Him. They are so in awe of what they are beholding that they remove their crowns of influence that have been placed on their heads every time to place at the holy feet of God. They do this because they know only He is superior and worthy enough to receive any praise, glory, or honor. Whatever they are feeling, experiencing, and witnessing with their eyes as they gaze at the throne of God causes every single part of their being to lay down before Him and give Him everything they have. Everything He gave them goes back to Him as an act of humility, awe, and honor.

I love the picture of this because it shows what is happening in the throne room of heaven for all of eternity. If we are seated in heavenly places, then we have the honor and privilege of joining in with all of heaven to magnify our King. There have been so many moments when I felt like I did not know what to do, when I didn't feel like worshiping or maybe I was heartbroken. As I began to worship God, it filled me with such faith and love and adoration for the One who always wins and always has the answer. It took my eyes off of me and what I was capable or incapable of in those moments and reminded me of who He is. My flesh was submitting to Jesus and His ways rather than my emotions, feelings, or thoughts. My spirit was coming into agreement with heaven. It gives you a heavenly perspective. Worship is all about God. It has nothing to do with us and what we can do and everything to do with us giving Him our everything because He is the worthy victor!

I was at a women's event in 2020 in Phoenix, and we were all worshiping the Lord together. I had been praying and believing for complete healing of my jaw. I was in pain 24/7 and experiencing discomfort. All of a sudden something clicked in my heart and head. I could feel the presence of God in the room and I knew He was showing up as the One who heals. The pain instantly left my jaw and has never returned. I showed up to give Him love and honor, and He zapped my jaw with His loving-kindness. What kind of King is this whom we get to serve and love on?

When we turn our hearts to God in worship, we become more aware of Him. Then we find that we are in the presence of our Father and we are ministering to Him and His incredibly perfect heart. I love seeing the worship gatherings that are popping up all around the United States. In 2020, Sean Feucht and my friends the Mauldins traveled around to magnify the man Jesus in major cities. This brought a reminder to all who were experiencing a lockdown that Jesus is King and Lord of our cities. Worship was filling the city with the sound of heaven and causing things to shift in the atmosphere.

The thousands who showed up looked to Jesus for our strength. I loved attending the one in Washington D.C. You could feel the glory of God in the National Mall as we magnified the man Jesus and prayed. I wept as people gave their lives to Jesus from this gathering. Salvation is the most beautiful and supernatural thing to witness. People struggling with suicide, lies, loneliness, depression, or who had never given their heart to the Lord were coming forward to give God their everything.

This is what was happening at these worship gatherings. People were getting healed. Oftentimes when we turn our hearts to Him in worship to give Him everything, there is something that tangibly pours back out from Him. In worship you are exalting Him and not asking for anything. Yet somehow, when God shows up, He comes as the healer, the comforter, the deliverer, the provider; the God who sees all comes into the hearts of the ones crying out before Him. He is in our midst, and heaven on earth will be the result.

> *Therefore let us be grateful for receiving a kingdom that cannot be shaken, and thus let us offer to God acceptable worship, with reverence and awe* (Hebrews 12:28 ESV).

This is a constant state of being for those who live on the narrow highway of holiness. There is no honor, privilege, gift, praise, or title that comes to us apart from God Himself. No battle ahead can be won without Him. We must learn how to come to Him and live from a place of reverence in every season of our life so that we never lose sight of the One who came to save all of mankind. The unshakable kingdom will demolish the shakable kingdoms of the earth, and we get to be part of this Holy Revolution that is rising up and will not be shaken. Protect your time in worship and live from this place for Him.

COMMUNION

Communion serves us as a powerful reminder of the death of our Jesus. He took it all on, unto death, so that we could live in this new covenant with Him. Then He showed us that death itself could not keep our Savior down. That same Spirit who breathed the breath of God right back into Him from such a dark void lives in each of us, and now we have no fear in death because we carry the resurrection life within.

> *Jesus said to them, "I am the bread of life; whoever comes to me shall not hunger, and whoever believes in me shall never thirst"* (John 6:35 ESV).

There are moments when I am holding communion and can't help but meditate on the body of our beloved Jesus. As I hold the bread in my hands, I think about every single pain, sickness, disease, whip, bruise, beating and more that He took on. It is very intense, I know, but it really helps me connect with the life of Jesus more. I keep allowing my imagination to go there and see as I meditate on His body. I can only imagine the cup of suffering He was drinking from as He took on every bit of darkness and sorrow. The most innocent, pure, and kind servant in the world took on all of it. What must have been going through His mind when people would spit on Him, laugh at Him, betray and accuse Him? Little did they know that what He was partaking in was also for them.

There in His body was pain, depression, hate, cancer, diseases and viruses of all kinds, death, fear, and more. He took on everything that was outside of our inheritance as holy and set apart ones so that we would be able to live a long and satisfying life with our beloved in eternity. He knew that those who partnered with Him would be able to do even greater things than we read about in the word through this new covenant. In order for this scripture to be accomplished, He went to the Father and sent His Spirit to show us how to live holy.

> *Very truly I tell you, whoever believes in me will do the works I have been doing, and they will do even greater things than these, because I am going to the Father* (John 14:12 NIV).

I begin to mediate on the blood of Jesus. I ponder on every vile and evil sin this gentle servant took on so that one day we could live holy as He lived holy. So that we could be reminded around the table of communion that He died so that we could live with Him for all of eternity. Repentance creeps into me as I begin to cry and confess anything and everything that I have done apart from Him. I grieve because of what He did on the cross to show me I did not have to live this way. Then I envision hope through the blood touching my body and wiping me clean of all sin and shame. Only He can make us clean. I never want to live a life in which my own spirit doesn't grieve within me at the taste or thought of sin. I never want to go a day without the leadership of His precious gift, the Holy Spirit. I want to be the living and breathing reward of His suffering through all of eternity. I cannot do this apart from a true depth of repentance and certainty that following Him is the only way.

This very act of communion around the table with others brings us together. I love what one of my spiritual moms, Briskilla, says, "Communion is like a blanket of unity that covers us." When I gather with others, it gives space for us to confess our sins as a family and break bread together around the very man who unites us all. We need one another, and breaking bread together brings unity that cannot be easily broken.

FASTING

You may want to close your book right now and stop reading at the thought of fasting, or you may be like me and absolutely love, love, love it. After all, Jesus did say, "*When* you fast." It's understood that fasting is part of our journey in following Him. I even consider it this way—if Jesus fasted and walked as close to the Father as He did, how much more should we?

> *When you fast, do not look somber as the hypocrites do, for they disfigure their faces to show others they are fasting. Truly I tell you, they have received their reward in full* (Matthew 6:16 NIV).

Remember when we talked earlier about those who give the appearance of godliness but are not actually inwardly living godly lives? Fasting is not a public service announcement unless a group of people decide to do it together. I would also like to say that every single time I have fasted, the Lord has given me more than enough energy to keep going and to be joyful. After all, fasting heightens every sense to the presence of God, and it's impossible to be disfigured in face when you're with Him—unless your face is glowing like Moses' was when he came down from the mountaintop, which is definitely on my bucket list.

Before I get to my personal testimonies of some fasts I have done, it would be silly of me not to mention some pretty epic examples we have all read in scripture. Ladies and gentlemen, the word of God is so woven with God's goodness and it's a blueprint that is still valuable and powerful today. Can we holler about Esther for a moment? Let's be real—when people throw around "such a time as this" about a career move or simple transition in their life, I don't think they realize the weight of that comment. Esther was born for "such a time as this" in that her entire life was on the line. She had no idea if she would find favor with the king in this moment of wanting to save an entire people group, so she laid down all of her ideas in the flesh to fast for three days and called her people to fast with her. She literally could have been killed by presenting herself to the king without being summoned by him. This fast allowed her and her people to rely completely on God for the victory as she was getting ready to approach the king with courage, favor, and love for her people.

Moses was with the Lord for 40 days and 40 nights and came out of that time with God with the Ten Commandments. The Ten Commandments are something we have followed for thousands of years. They have helped us discern the goodness of God in a world that has fallen. These commandments were revealed to someone just like you and me who took the time to let go of all of the desires of the flesh to be with God for 40 days and came out of that time with something as transformative and epic as the Ten Commandments. Are you with me here?

If that's not enough to get you excited about fasting, the Holy Spirit led Jesus into the wilderness for 40 days and 40 nights to fast and wrestle with the enemy. In Matthew 4:1 of *The Passion Translation* it says that the Holy Spirit led him there to "reveal his strength against the accuser by going through the ordeal of testing." Jesus himself came out of a 40-day fast in the Judaea desert and went face to face with satan. The temptation level that was presented in that conversation is crazy. Jesus didn't waver from God's heart and character during the time of temptation. Angels came and ministered to Jesus' needs, and He walked into His time of ministry out of this fast. You could also be walking out of a fast into your epic time of ministry. Do you realize the power of fasting yet?

I love fasting because it is intense and beautiful at the same time. There are so many different types of fasts that we read about in the word of God. You can fast from food, social media, television, eating out, and the list goes on and on. You can fast for three days, one day, 21 days, 40 days, or a year. There is no formula. This is always something I am speaking to Holy Spirit about because He will often highlight things to me that I could give up for a certain amount of time. I may have a deep desire to give the Lord things that I love for a given amount of time so that I can lean into Him without distraction.

Most importantly, I believe the crucial part of a fast is that you are led by the Holy Spirit on it and not a formula you have seen. I love the examples in the word of God, but I also want to encourage you to experience the leadership of the Holy One when you step into a time of fasting like these wonderful heroes of faith did. Allow the Holy Spirit to lead you all throughout each day of your fast and you will experience something epic.

MY FIRST FAST

When I was in college, I was elected into a position of leadership in my sorority that I knew was from the Lord. I really wanted to bring unity among a group of 120 women God's way. I felt like I needed to lay things I loved down because I really needed God's help and wanted to focus in on Him. I remember taking all sugar and bread out of my diet until the final show I was directing because I did not want food to distract me from hearing the Lord and leading well. I knew I was fasting, but I didn't really know what that meant, so this was all in faith for me. I just knew that I loved food too much and wanted to give God the things that could possibly allow me to think poorly of myself or not be wholeheartedly aware of Him as my strength.

During this time I prayed for each girl in the show and wrote them a handwritten letter. I wanted them to know that I loved them and that I believed in them. In turn, it gave me eyes to see them from God's heart. I wanted to be aware of God during this time because I wanted everything I said to be in love, unity, and excellence. We had lost seven years in a row in this competitive production, and when I came in and directed as a junior, we won! It was absolutely amazing. However, the best part about it was the unity that our sorority needed to be able to function as a group of sisters. There was some major division going on, and I knew only Jesus could create a moment for us to be and feel unified again.

I prayed over *everything* in that show. I even thanked God for the thread that was on sale for our costumes at the time because I knew that was just another way of Him being there for us. I fasted because I wanted to let go of my fleshly desires and see unity, and we saw it by the end of the fast. This was between me and the Lord. I was more aware of God, more in love with Him, and more sensitive to His love for others because I was setting time aside to pray for these women each night. Let me just say, that fast was incredibly worth it. I was in the word, praying for people, and looking completely outside of myself to see His goodness in His people. I was spending heaps of time with the Father, relying on Him for help, and it was transformative. It made me realize this spiritual principle was valuable. I learned to recognize God and give thanks in all circumstances, and I came out stronger in the Lord.

NOT ALWAYS IMMEDIATE

I have not always seen the fruit of fasts immediately following. In August of 2013, I did a liquid fast for marriages and families in our church. I invited the staff to join me, and Sharla, who is like a spiritual mother to me, said "yes" to this wonderful endeavor. I felt so grieved by what we were hearing about the marriages in our congregation that I knew we needed to come before the Lord for more breakthrough. Sharla and I prayed every day for different couples, and we also prayed every day for one specific couple. We knew during this fast that we might not see the fruit of our prayers during it, but we would see it one day. The crazy part is that the relationship we covered the most during this time took a turn for the worst.

My friend's husband of over 30 years wanted a divorce. Papers were put on the table, yet we did not give up and we did not give in to what we saw. Fasting allowed us to hear God and stand in that place until we saw His desire happen. The best part here is that within a year of the separation they were back together happily and in a supernatural way. This man is one of the kindest men you'll ever meet, and his wife is one whose name you would read about in modern-day scripture because of the unwavering faith she has in God.

Her husband was an unbeliever through the entire marriage, and when they came back together he slowly started to ask more about the Lord and is now attending a church near their home. In December of 2020, he chose to get baptized in the lake outside their home. Remember, this fast took place in 2013, and in 2020 he got baptized. I know with all my heart that the fast Sharla and I did made a difference. This fast also matured us in our faith to believe for what we could not see rather than what could be seen.

Fasting is an intimate and beautiful time with God. He will reveal things to you in this place as you silence everything around you to see what He is doing, hear what He is saying, and bring understanding with it.

My hope is that your heart is hungrier and more open to communion, thanksgiving, worship, and fasting with Him. I believe these keys will help us stay in love with our beloved Jesus. I also believe they will help us stay grounded and rooted in the assignments we each have as the Holy Revolution continues to rise and grow on the earth. After all, Jesus Himself did each of these things when He walked the earth. What a joy to drink from the same cup.

PRAYER

Lord, would You lead me in creative ways to connect even more with You? I want to know You more and discover Your character and Your dreams on earth. Lead me in thanksgiving, lead me in worship, and please lead me in fasting. I want to know You more. Thank You for Your love and Your leadership. I belong to You. Amen.

Chapter 8

THE WARRIOR'S HEART

Love the Lord your God with all your heart and with all your soul and with all your mind and with all your strength.

—MARK 12:30 NIV

This first commandment doesn't say love the Lord your God with part of your heart and part of your soul and part of your mind. No, it says to love Him with *all* of it. That means that we are to give Him all that is within us. That we recognize Him as the leader of all our emotions, thoughts, beliefs, and being. Everything we do is in submission to Him. We serve the one true Master. If the thought of "serving a master" doesn't line up well with you, I would ask if you've met this one yet. To become a slave to Christ is to actually live an abundant life and to discover who you were created to be all along.

As men and women in this Holy Revolution, it is our choice and our job to steward our hearts well in order to accomplish all the Lord has for us. Jesus cares more about your heart than your actions. So many times we read that if we don't have love in our hearts then nothing we do has any weight or meaning to it.

THE HEART

Each time the Lord showed me someone in the encounter I shared in Chapter 1, He showed me how He loves us perfectly, whole and untainted. It has caused me to realize that guarding my heart is far more important than anything else. It is stored up within Him and not anything or anyone we could find in this world. The crazy part is, when we turn our hearts completely and fully to Him is the moment when everything in our life changes.

> *The Lord your God will circumcise your hearts and the hearts of your descendants, so that you may love him with all your heart and with all your soul, and live* (Deuteronomy 30:6 NIV).

He removes the darkness, the funk, the lies, the deceit, the destruction. Do you understand the power of turning your heart to Him? This means *He* comes and delivers us and takes away everything that makes it impure, and the blessings that come from this are absolutely crazy. However, it is a choice for us to do this. He never makes us; He always has an open invitation as long as we have breath in our lungs to serve Him. As we turn our hearts to Him, he reveals all of the darkness that gets in the way of us being completely surrendered so that nothing can keep us from Him. Then, we allow Him to remove it by tearing down the false idols and gods within our hearts and replacing them with His truth only.

STORING UP

A good man brings good things out of the good stored up in his heart, and an evil man brings evil things out of the evil stored up in his heart. For the mouth speaks what the heart is full of (Luke 6:45 NIV).

You can see the treasures of a person by what is stored in their heart. It comes out of their mouth and bleeds into every action they take on earth. Jesus even says in Matthew 12:34, "For from the overflow of the heart the mouth speaks" (TLV). He continues in this chapter to talk about the weight of our words and how one day we will be held accountable for everything we have said. This should strike us with the fear of the Lord. God will be addressing what we chose to say from our mouths one day. If what is coming out of our mouth is not bringing life, then we need to reevaluate what we are letting in. This is the overflow from our hearts coming out of our mouths. So if evil, malice, gossip, doubt, and slander are coming out of our mouths, where are we allowing that to enter in? We must repent immediately and then cut it off at the root and replace it with the holy love of God.

Are you listening to what's coming out of your mouth and aware of what actions you are taking? The battle first starts within ourselves before we are to look at it in others. It's not hard to see the fruit of one's life when they face a difficult circumstance as shaking comes. You can see it in what the person puts their time into and values. Is it pure, clean, and holy? Are their words toward others kind, gentle, and patient? I encourage you to invite the Holy Spirit in to lead you here. Ask Him to help make you aware of what is coming out of your mouth and why.

TURNING OUR HEARTS TO HIM ALONE

We carry within us a powerful threat of inheritance that'll cause the enemy to disperse, run, and flee before our very eyes. The Lord has delivered the enemy time and time again into the hands of the righteous ones whose hearts were turned to Him. Their hearts were turned to Him because they knew the character and nature of our victor in heaven. They knew the battle belonged to the Lord, not to them.

*For the eyes of the Lord range throughout
the earth to strengthen those whose hearts*

*are fully committed to him. You have done
a foolish thing, and from now on you will
be at war* (2 Chronicles 16:9 NIV).

A prophet spoke the above words to King Asa. King Asa was a leader who experienced the Lord delivering the enemy into his hands supernaturally time and time again. He was a king who made God Israel's Lord, and God was magnified throughout the land. Toward the end of King Asa's life, he relied on King Aram and not the Lord. When King Asa chose to rely on human strength rather than God, the result was that the country would be at war for 70 years. Think about this—his whole life he served the Lord, and one time of turning to man created this big of a war within his people.

Our decisions make a bigger impact than we know. When our hearts are submitted to Jesus as Lord, He strengthens us and wins the battles ahead. He strengthens us because we cannot accomplish His plans for us in our own strength. Much of the time the battles before us look impossible and will require such surrender to and trust in the Lord that we know we cannot move from that place, no matter the cost. I have found by reading about the life of King Asa that when my heart is turned to me, I am at war with myself. When my heart is turned to others for strength in a way that it was not created to, I am at war with them. He gives us peace and the world gives us war.

Whatever we are turned to will be the fruit of war or peace. Life or death.

I am also moved by the kings of the Old Testament who lived evil their whole lives and, in a moment, genuinely turned their hearts to the Lord in true repentance. God met them with mercy rather than judgment. It saved them and their entire nation. Their response to this place of turning their hearts to God was going into their country and tearing down every high place, idol, and false god that the people exalted high above our God. This is true repentance and a true picture of a heart being fully committed to Him. It's never too late for us and it's never too late for those we have been praying for to turn to Him.

We need to pray for the hearts of others rather than complain and criticize about their weaknesses. If we criticize them, we lose the authority to speak into their lives and lose the privilege to watch God turn their hearts to Jesus. It is truly never too late for us and it's never too late for those around us. I keep repeating this because this is the heart of a true, holy warrior in this hour.

The men and women around you need to see you stand always in submission to Jesus. People are watching us and people are impacted greatly by the way we choose to position our hearts. It could be your children, your ministry, your employees, your students, your friends, your spiritual children, and those who are watching you more than you know who will be impacted deeply by your decision to not move from the place of serving Jesus with *all* of your heart.

WITH ALL VIGILANCE

Keep your heart with all vigilance, for from it flow the springs of life (Proverbs 4:23 ESV).

Merriam-Webster defines *vigilant* as "alertly watchful especially to avoid danger." The Lord calls us to watch our heart to avoid any danger. He gave me a picture one time that taught me how to guard my heart. Much of the time, for me, it's the thoughts that come into my mind because of the depression I battled off and on for over a decade. I see myself as a beautiful, clean home that Jesus lives in with me. It used to be that these ugly thoughts would knock on the door and I would bring them into my home and entertain them for a very long time. Then, when Jesus delivered me and evicted all of the evil from my home, I became a clean house. There was a time when they would knock and I learned not to answer, even though it was tempting. Then I could sense them in my front yard, and I would not allow them on the grass. Then I realized the value of me living in a gated community because mama ain't got time for those kinds of demons and lies to come living inside her. This house belongs to the Lord. Therefore, having a gated community where my home dwells keeps my heart from any evil.

I want to get really real here, but before I dive in with you please keep in mind that this comes down to the leadership of the Holy Spirit and being madly in love with the man Jesus. Holy Spirit and the word will always show us what this means, and this is to help stir a healthy dialogue with you and Him. So let's get real here with some examples. For many of us it's who we are following or what we are searching for on social media. What is the post displaying visually and then what is it actually leading you to? Is it sexual in nature? Is it causing jealousy or envy? Are you all of a sudden wishing you had some designer brands to fit in more?

What about the TV shows we are watching? Are they cursing all the time, normalizing behavior and lifestyles that the Lord deems as unholy? What about the movies you are allowing in? Are those movies normalizing sinful behavior with no redeeming quality to holiness? I used to do that and realized that needed to stop. There are many times that men and women who love the Lord encourage me to watch shows or movies that they say are pure. I learned quickly that my husband and I need to do the research before we even view it, because everyone's standards are different from my own. So Lance and I look up the details of any inappropriate behavior in movies or shows to ensure that we are protecting all the eye and ear gates.

Let's talk about humor for a moment. What are we laughing at? I used to find cursing really funny back in the day. I also thought jokes that were really inappropriate were hilarious and would even make them myself. Now, these types of jokes grieve my heart because of how guarded I have become with my heart. What about fashion? I am really big on wearing what I genuinely love. Being in love with Jesus has caused me to have a reverence for even the way I dress. Is the way I am dressed holy and pure? Am I putting too much of myself out there in this outfit, and what can I do to present myself as pure and holy as He has called me to be?

Let's take it a step further. What about the people you are allowing into your heart and spending time with? Are they ones who help sharpen you and encourage you to keep living holy, or do you find it harder to live a lifestyle of holiness with them close by? Are they honoring about people who are not around? I am not telling you to throw these people out to the curb. I am asking, are they in your inner circle and do you need different inner circle friends who inspire you and empower you to know Jesus more? Our friendships matter and they also affect our heart.

GUARDING YOUR HEART AND MIND

But I tell you that anyone who looks at a woman lustfully has already committed adultery with her in his heart (Matthew 5:28 NIV).

Are you ready for the big kicker here? This is where I am so grateful for the deep level of freedom and joy that Jesus has delivered me into. Our thoughts are as real, powerful, and weighty as our actions. What?! Our thoughts affect our hearts and come from them. I used to live in critical city in my head before I realized the true gift of discernment. Oftentimes, I could see things going on in people's lives and it would frustrate me or I would put up a wall toward them, and neither of those options were love. True discernment is when we grieve because of darkness in other people's lives and we can pray for them or do as the Lord leads us to in those moments with maturity and courage. It doesn't change the way you see them from the Lord's heart. He gives true discerners an aerial view of people, and it fills us with love. Jesus desires us to be liberated even in our thoughts.

Our thoughts of internal dialogue are great indicators of how sick or whole our hearts are. Keep the word flowing within and be quick to repent of any evil thought you have toward yourself or toward others. If you are fantasizing about immoral situations in your head, take it to the Holy One and ask Him what He has to say. Hand Him the thought and be quick to repent here. When you repent, ask Him to fill that place where evil was held with His truth and His peace. Do not allow those thoughts to come back. Throw them in the trash and build a habit of purity within. It is 100 percent our choice what we put our mind to and it does require diligence to overcome. The good news is that you don't have to overcome alone. He already overcame those thoughts and isn't afraid of getting in your mess with you to pull you back into truth. Will you let Him?

Sin flows from a heart that is not fully committed to the Lord. This is why it is absolutely important to fill our hearts with Him and take very seriously our call to protect every gate the Lord has given to us.

> *For to set the mind on the flesh is death,*
> *but to set the mind on the Spirit is life and*
> *peace* (Romans 8:6 ESV).

Remember, focusing on the sins in our lives to try to overcome will not lead to life. Plot twist—we are not God and we never will be. He has left us the Holy Spirit who consistently leads us to Jesus. They will always lead us to life and peace. Sin will always lead to death. Every day we are faced with life or death from the smallest to the biggest of ways. This is why thankfulness is so important and can break off the poopy thoughts and rewire us to be more aware of Him. After all, it does say that we enter His gates with thanksgiving in our hearts. So let us be thankful so that we can remain in His gates and not the gates of ourselves as lord.

We can also rewire our thoughts to enjoy the simple disciplines of life. I remember in college I really disliked running. It just wasn't fun for me at all. One day,

I decided I was going to start meditating on how much I loved it while running, to see if it would help me. I would tell myself in my thoughts, "You are such a powerful runner, Jamie Lyn. I was made for this. Lord, thank You for making me a strong runner. Jamie Lyn, you're almost there." Believe it or not, this helped me enjoy running, and I began to run longer and longer distances. Our thoughts can be rewired from bad ones to good ones. What do you need a new perspective on in the thought patterns of your heart?

THE POWER OF OUR WORDS

It's important to remember how impactful the words are when they leave our mouths. I love the story in Matthew 21 when Jesus is walking by the fig tree. He finds that it isn't bearing any fruit and curses it with His words as He tells the tree it will never bear fruit again. The fig tree shriveled up immediately and the disciples were shocked. They were amazed by what they just saw and asked, "How did that happen so quickly?" Jesus responded with the following:

> *Truly I tell you, if you have faith and do not doubt, not only can you do what was done to the fig tree, but also you can say to this mountain, "Go, throw yourself into the sea," and it will be done. If you believe, you will receive whatever you ask for in prayer* (Matthew 21:21-22 NIV).

If we truly believe in our hearts that the word is true and God means exactly what He says then our mouths will flow with powerful decrees, with love, with blessings, and with life. We will cast out darkness, and we will watch heaven invade earth. If we believe toxic lies in our heart and begin to curse people with our words, then that's what we will see handed to us and the situations we are in. Trust me, I was an expert in the life of depression, remember? It was so bad that I will help fight to make sure no one else lives in the land of doubt and curses ever again.

> *Open your mouth with a mighty decree;*
> *I will fulfill it now, you'll see! The words*
> *that you speak, so shall it be!* (Psalm 81:10 TPT)

My friends and mentors Patricia King and Sandy Ross have taught thousands of men and women the power of a decree. What you believe, you say. What you say, you get. I love hearing everyday examples that Sandy gives as she preaches. She responds to people in a way that allows them to really hear what they are saying. Are you declaring life or are you declaring death over your circumstance? Because that is what you're going to get. It causes men and women to dig into the word, listen to what the Lord is saying about a situation, and decree, decree, decree until they believe it and until they see it happen. This requires diligence and self-control to get to a place where you respond with the sound of heaven rather than agree with what the world says.

This is why it is so vital that we get the word of God in us so that in moments when the shaking comes we will have the word of God bubbling out of our lips. We have the power and authority, when we believe, to speak life to the tree that isn't bearing any fruit and watch it bear fruit. Are you following me here? These words are powerful, and what we have stored up in our hearts will come out.

> *The tongue has the power of life and death, and those who love it will eat its fruit* (Proverbs 18:21 NIV).

So what tree are you eating from today? Are you feeding on the news that is instilling fear, lies, and hopelessness to everyone tuning in? If you are, then that will be the overflow of your heart. You are a tree, and whatever you are watering your heart with is what you will water other hearts with. Are you eating from the tree of life in relationship with God and in His word? If so, you will be able to decree and see what God is doing and saying and pour that into other people's hearts when they need it.

NEVER RETURNING VOID

> *So shall my word be that goes out from my mouth; it shall not return to me empty, but it shall accomplish that which*

*I purpose, and shall succeed in the thing
for which I sent it* (Isaiah 55:11 ESV).

When the Lord speaks, it is like pouring water out
of a pitcher and into the root system of what He is
speaking to. It flows out and into the designated place
for watering. It does not flow from the roots and back
into the pitcher. So is the power of words. They go to
what you are speaking to and accomplish the mission.

We must learn to share the good news and exercise
this gift of changing the atmosphere on a daily basis.
Speaking has everything to do with releasing the
sound of heaven so that others may know Him. When
we begin to understand that people's lives could literally be changed forever because we choose to decree
the word of God and that the entire atmosphere shifts
around us with life, the fear that tried to knock begins
to dwindle and evaporate as courage carries us past it.

*And God said, "Let there be light," and
there was light* (Genesis 1:3 NIV).

The Lord made each of us in His image. When He
spoke and used His audible voice, creation came into
being. He said "let there be light" and there was light.
He then began to speak to the heavens and the earth to
put them in their places and give them a name. When
He did these things, they were as He said. His voice
changed everything to form what He was declaring.
This means our words carry much power and we have

the ability to speak life or death into the atmosphere as image bearers of God.

When I was delivered from endometriosis, I was saying a prayer out loud at a huge deliverance/prayer meeting. I began to feel something choking my neck, and my body began to shake all over. It was a time when I could feel light come into my body and rip darkness out and fill it with the kingdom of heaven. I could feel something moving from my ovaries, where endometriosis is, up my body, and out of my mouth. I remember being embarrassed, but I also remember I didn't care because I wanted healing and it was happening. Something did not want me to say this prayer out loud and gave me a sobering taste of how important speaking was.

I pushed through and received my healing in Jesus by saying the prayer out loud anyway. This was another one of those moments when I knew God was real because I could never have created a moment like this. This healing taught me about the power of my words because the enemy was wanting to choke me so I couldn't speak. Don't let him choke you by remaining silent or by speaking death over yourself or others. This will be a huge test in the Holy Revolution.

When you find yourself in a situation moving forward that seems dark or hopeless, it is time to formulate an official order from heaven to earth. Did the doctor give you terminal news? What will you believe in your heart and decree with your mouth? Does a family member seem to be running further and further away from the Lord? It's time to formulate decrees and say them every day. Decrees are not a time to be manipulative and decree what you want. A decree is an official order issued by a legal authority. Decrees are words that you receive from the Lord in scriptures or from Him directly over a situation. They are the heart and will of the Father declared. It's important to hold these decrees in our hearts until we believe and keep praying them through and decreeing them until we see it happen.

When I was depressed, my thoughts and words were horrible toward myself. I was marinating in dark and made-up news each night I was alone. When I was set free, I was marinating in God's truth and decreeing His good word. I have learned that what I say, pray, and decree creates something in the natural. Words water something, and I want that water to be pure and holy.

So what do you need to see shift today? Get in the word and decree those scriptures out loud. Believe it in your heart and decree it out loud. We need your voice in the secret place and in our communities with the sound of holiness flowing out of you. Your words can literally bring healing to someone's body and life. Your words can help shift a nation.

Prayer for a Healthy Heart

Father, I thank You for creating me for this time. If there is anything that I am allowing into my heart that is affecting me negatively, I thank You for revealing it to me. If there is anything I am in agreement with that is not true, I thank You for extracting it and replacing it with Your truth. Father, thank You for helping me steward my heart well and speak powerful things out of this mouth You gave me. I declare that my voice and my lips will speak of Your love forever and ever, amen.

Chapter 9

THE SEPARATION

He is separating us within the body of Christ. In 2017, when I had the encounter I shared in the first chapter, I wept a lot. I would weep at the slightest thought of people not giving Him their everything. I wept because I tasted, could feel and see the depth of worthiness He carries for us to lay our everything down. I wept because I wanted to give Him everything I had. How could we miss even the tiny moments of opportunity to be with Him? So many have become desensitized to the moments when He is presenting Himself to us, and now it doesn't take too long to see in our world that the separation has come.

> *No one can serve two masters, for either he will hate the one and love the other, or he will be devoted to the one and despise the other. You cannot serve God and money* (Matthew 6:24 ESV).

I remember seeing men and women in the church who genuinely believed they had given Jesus their everything but were too caught up in doing things their way and providing for themselves. They didn't even know they needed more of Him because they had everything they needed in the natural.

They looked at those who were weeping on the floor, giving Jesus their all in worship, and in their hearts said, "I don't want that or need that." Some were worship leaders on a platform, the youth leaders, the business owners, the teachers, and the list could go on. It could have been anyone in the room, and it could be any of us. Let's be honest, I have been that person before. We cannot serve both masters, and when we serve something that isn't Jesus we are deceived. The catchy part about deception is those who are deceived don't know they are.

Humility will be a treasure and a powerful characteristic of this revolution. It will require humility in order for the Holy Spirit to reveal to us what we are believing that is keeping us from serving Jesus and Jesus only.

THE APPEARANCE OF GODLINESS

We are living in a time when it is so easy for people to build their platforms, as previously mentioned. However, we must be aware of those who have the appearance of godliness but are not actually godly. The word of God talks about the days that we are facing now and lists things that people will be walking in who have the appearance of loving Him but do not love Him.

> *But understand this, that in the last days there will come times of difficulty. For people will be lovers of self, lovers of money, proud, arrogant, abusive, disobedient to their parents, ungrateful, unholy, heartless, unappeasable, slanderous, without self-control, brutal, not loving good, treacherous, reckless, swollen with conceit, lovers of pleasure rather than lovers of God, having the appearance of godliness, but denying its power. Avoid such people* (2 Timothy 3:1-5 ESV).

Are you in a place where you can read this scripture above and genuinely be self-aware enough to know whether you are walking in one or more of these things? I know I have walked in many of these. A religious spirit is one that appears to be godly, checks off the list of attending church on a Sunday, and to the outside world they look like they have it all together. Yet inside they are burning with the desire and lust of flesh, and those without discernment can be easily fooled. I remember these days of loving money, being ungrateful, unholy, and denying God's power. Days without humility, when I was not hungry to grow by receiving correction from the Father. I was not repenting of these wicked ways, and I was choosing a path of destruction. Can you relate?

It is dangerous to preach holiness without repentance, and even the way repentance is preached is very key. I look at the life of John the Baptist. He prepared a way for everyone to receive Jesus by preaching, "Repent, for the kingdom of heaven is at hand" (Matt. 3:2 ESV). It's profoundly laid out in sequence.

First, we have John the Baptist leading the way with repentance and baptism, followed by Jesus coming to baptize everyone in the Holy Spirit and fire. In order to really walk with Jesus, we must first repent. John the Baptist even pointed to the religious leaders and warned them that they must produce fruit in keeping with repentance. True repentance comes with a life that is constantly being transformed by the presence of God, and the fruit of our lives will show this.

Jesus' first message that He preached after being baptized was repentance. When we repent, we are choosing to walk on the path of becoming more like Him; it does not mean that we must strive to be perfect. However, if we want to be filled with the Holy Spirit and walk in the ways of God, it starts with repentance.

I see a generation in you and me who invites the Holy Spirit in to reveal areas where we have built walls that keep us from walking close with Him. When He gently and kindly reveals these areas to us, we repent. We turn to Him and say, "Father, please forgive me for walking in (insert here). This is not who You created me to be and I desire to be led by You. Please take this from me and lead me in Your ways." There are a number of ways to repent, but repentance is something that once you apologize, you move forward and away from those things. He forgives us and wipes the slate clean.

Those with good character walk on a smooth path, with no detour or deviation. But the wicked keep falling because of their own wickedness (Proverbs 11:5 TPT).

Once God gave me a picture of sin that changed my world. He showed me a toddler walking. You know the stage when they constantly look like they are walking downhill? When they trip or fall their parents do not scream at them and punish them. They encourage them to get up and keep walking. There are moments when we have tripped and sinned—whether living in doubt, putting something before God, being critical, cursing, slandering others, etc.—while we are growing in our maturity as Christians. In these moments, I can feel the grief of the Holy Spirit (conviction), and He reminds me of who I am and encourages me to get up (repent) and keep walking toward God. I have never heard God scream angrily at me. I have always been met by His kindness. This picture of me growing in my walk allowed me to extend grace to myself and others the same way God does.

This does not mean that I can keep sinning. In fact, His love and grace empower us to live a life set apart away from sin. When I mess up, I quickly run to my Father in heaven and apologize. Every single time I am met with love, kindness, and forgiveness. Do you realize how many times He has forgiven me? Experiencing this kind of love and forgiveness has allowed me to love and forgive others who wrong me as well. I want them to experience God's kindness and not satan's condemnation.

Jesus showed us that holiness protects us from evil. Will we be tempted? Yes; He was. However, when we are walking with God every day and protecting every entry point of our lives from evil, we will be able to be part of "the wheat" that we are going to dive more into.

THE WHEAT AND THE TARE

I was sitting on an airplane reading my Bible when all of a sudden these things popped out to me about the wheat and the tare regarding separation. I want to start by saying, as a creative artist, this is what I saw for this parable that I wanted to encourage you in as I sought wisdom.

> He answered, "The one who sowed the good seed is the Son of Man. The field is the world, and the good seed stands for the people of the kingdom. The weeds are the people of the evil one, and the enemy who sows them is the devil. The harvest is

*the end of the age, and the harvesters are
angels"* (Matthew 13:37-39 NIV).

Jesus sowed good seed into us by preaching, teaching, and leading us. He has sent us out into the world
via the great commission to grow and plant these
seeds in others. The devil sows seed as well. His seeds
are sin, and one day the harvesters are coming to harvest the field. Who does it say is going to harvest? His
angels. Not you and not me. I am not talking about the
harvest we get to bring in. This is different. Hear me
out here and let's keep reading.

> *As the weeds are pulled up and burned in
> the fire, so it will be at the end of the age.
> The Son of Man will send out his angels,
> and they will weed out of his kingdom
> everything that causes sin and all who do
> evil. They will throw them into the blazing
> furnace, where there will be weeping and
> gnashing of teeth. Then the righteous will
> shine like the sun in the kingdom of their
> Father. Whoever has ears, let them hear*
> (Matthew 13:40-43 NIV).

Jesus will send out His angels to "weed out of His
kingdom everything that causes sin and all who do
evil." There will be a fire they are thrown into—like
lukewarm water spit out of the mouth, eh? Then, the
righteous will replace them. We have seen the exposure
of influential leaders in the church, with government

officials, with people who work with us in business, and more. Okay, before we break this down more let's also check out this part of the parable:

> *Jesus told them another parable: "The kingdom of heaven is like a man who sowed good seed in his field. But while everyone was sleeping, his enemy came and sowed weeds among the wheat, and went away. When the wheat sprouted and formed heads, then the weeds also appeared"* (Matthew 13:24-26 NIV).

WHERE ARE WE SLEEPING?

This parable is amazing. Imagine you created the most beautiful painting in the world and it was a prized treasure to you. You worked so hard on it, and then one night you leave the art studio unlocked and a stranger breaks in and pours black paint all over it. Dramatic, I know, but why was the art studio not locked? There are areas of our lives where we cannot afford to be asleep. We cannot afford to leave the doors unlocked to the areas of our lives that God has deemed a treasure. Do not let the enemy have access to places and spaces of your heart by not being mindful.

I am a creative, so one of the big areas for me is what I am watching and listening to. When I hear things, I am very visual and what I see affects me for the better or for worse. If I am not guarding my eyes and ears on TV or in movies, then I am opening my eye and ear gates that lead straight to my heart. If I allow the enemy to sow a seed of lust into my heart, it will grow. What about all my married people? Ever have a conversation with someone of the opposite sex who gives you attention in a way that your significant other doesn't give you? Do not allow yourself to sleep here. You must protect your heart and be real and authentic with God in those places. Don't let them keep coming into a space they were not made to be in. That's how the beginning seeds of affairs are planted when we are not watchful. We cannot let both masters into our heart because we can only have one or the other.

> *Know the importance of the season you're in and a wise son you will be. But what a waste when an incompetent son sleeps through his day of opportunity!* (Proverbs 10:5 TPT)

Is there an area of your life where you may be hitting the snooze button or allowing yourself to slumber when the Lord has called you to protect it and stay vigilant? In Proverbs it talks about the importance of staying awake during the harvest rather than sleeping through it. I love when Jesus came out of His time in the desert with the Holy Spirit. He stood face to face with satan and, because He was watchful and filled with God's truth, the enemy could not sow evil into His life with the temptations of lies he offered. We are called to do the same—fill our hearts with prayer and His word. Stay watchful and allow Him to lead us. The tares will entertain evil and allow the enemy to keep sowing seed. The wheat will protect the fields of their hearts and help others do the same.

LET HIS PEOPLE GROW

So, let's finish out this mind-blowing parable. The servants came running to their master and asked him if they should pull the weeds out from the harvest, and this was His response:

> "No," he answered, "because while you are pulling the weeds, you may uproot the wheat with them. Let both grow together until the harvest. At that time I will tell the harvesters: First collect the weeds and tie them in bundles to be burned; then gather the wheat and bring it into my barn" (Matthew 13:29-30 NIV).

Wheat and tare look the same while they are growing until they have both reached full maturity. Remember it said "when the wheat sprouted and formed heads, the weeds also appeared." When you begin to see good fruit in your life, the enemy is also lurking and wanting to manifest his ugly head around you somewhere. You got a promotion and jealousy pops up from a friend who chooses to slander you. Someone else is getting married and you have been praying for that for yourself and you feel jealous and it's hard for you to celebrate with them. Maybe you just purchased a new home and all of a sudden your spouse lost their job. The enemy is out to kill, steal, and destroy as we all know. He doesn't like celebrating others and loves making those weeds grow wherever he can.

This is where humility really comes in. Is someone else doing what you have always longed to do and you think you should be doing it more than they should? Do you feel that poopy-ness stirring within you? Are others coming at you with negativity, accusation, and evil while you're growing in your spiritual gifts? Did you deliver a pure message and people who don't know you are taking it out of context? It's how we choose to respond in these moments that helps produce that wonderful, heavy fruit in our lives. The more faithful you are with your heart before God in these moments, the quicker you will grow and mature.

THE FRUIT

Another thing that I learned about this parable with wheat and tares is that tares, at maturity, lack substance and they stand up tall and proud. There are small seeds in the tares that cause dizziness and nausea if you eat them. You know that person who just seems to be toxic? They can't stop gossiping, slandering, bragging about themselves, getting drunk, or sleeping around? Someone who lacks humility to grow? They could even brag about these things if they have gone deep enough into them. These people are really hard to be around. Have you been this person to others before?

I did not always know what to do around these people, but I have learned more and more that this doesn't mean they will be a tare. I thought, in my heart, it meant they were a lost cause when I was younger and I needed to avoid them at all costs. When I was that way, others were patient with me and helped me learn how to grow in God. Now, I can do the same for them. If I can extend grace and truth in these moments then it could help them grow. It also said that the angels would come and pick the wheat out from the tare. This was an "aha" moment of realizing I wasn't created to judge where someone was going to choose to go or what path they were going to choose to take. I definitely want to make sure that I am inviting as many people as possible into the lifestyle of being wheat, but I cannot control who chooses.

As we are all growing and maturing in the Lord, we each face different battles. We don't have to face them alone. Be bold and courageous with your friends. First, pray and ask Jesus what His heart and desires are for them. Once you get that aerial view of the situation, ask for wisdom on how to approach them. There are times when these conversations have happened so many times, and they are not willing to hear it because of pride. I am led to walk away, as it says in Second Timothy 3, "to avoid such people," and I am grieved every single time, and others I am a little relieved because it was so hard and painful. They may just be the tare, or maybe someone else will come along and be the one who sees them repent and choose Jesus. Other times, they are grateful that someone would love them in this way. Don't stop praying for them. Also remember, it doesn't mean you have to keep hanging out with them.

The wheat is heavier at maturity. The weight of their fruit causes them to bow in humility. I love this about wheat. It reminds me of Paul. Paul was flipping awesome. He always boasted in his weakness because he knew he could only overcome the world by the power of Jesus Christ. We have each been given gifts naturally and supernaturally from God. These are from Him and should always be given and stewarded before Him.

When we get promoted, it's because of Him and we can boast in His faithfulness. When we get accurate prophetic words, we can boast in the Lord because He shared them with us. I am not talking about walking in false humility where you constantly say, "It's the Lord, brother," every time someone compliments you. It's good to say, "Thank you," and walk straight over to the Lord with thanksgiving because you know that gift was from Him to begin with. The Holy Spirit is amazing at walking in humility. He always points us to the man Jesus when He shows up. One of many perfect characteristics of the Holy One.

CORRECTION IS PROTECTION

They disciplined us for a little while as they thought best; but God disciplines us for our good, in order that we may share in his holiness (Hebrews 12:10 NIV).

Speaking of humility, correction is one of my biggest love languages. We need to surround ourselves with people who don't tell us what we want to hear, but who tell us what we need to hear. In a world where we do face this modern-day battle of influencers and platform builders, we must learn the value of correction. This is a standard in my closest relationships, and I know someone loves me when they have the courage to protect me by correcting me. I have grown to love this because I leaned in when it was painful and realized the fruit and growth that comes from these moments are for my protection and freedom. Still to this day, it stings to hear it initially but it stings so good for someone to remind you of who God created you to be.

While we are growing in our spiritual gifts and character, we will need that compass of the Holy Spirit to lead us into truth. There will be times when the course needs some redirection in our thoughts, hearts, or friendships. It is vital for us to continue posturing ourselves in a place where we can hear the Holy Spirit bring correction. He only shares what the Father is sharing with Him, so do not let those words fall to the ground but let them water your heart.

> *For the moment all discipline seems painful rather than pleasant, but later it yields the peaceful fruit of righteousness to those who have been trained by it* (Hebrews 12:11 ESV).

If we keep ignoring Him where we need to be corrected, eventually we will fall, and the fall will be the size of our platform. If we become a massive influencer, that pride from the enemy that we kept ignoring will begin to grow bigger and bigger because we are sleeping on protecting our hearts. The spirit of lust that the Holy Spirit has been encouraging us to let go of will grow and become darker, and that thing can lead to the darkest night of a person's soul and broadcast for all to see. We have seen these massive church leaders and Hollywood stars fall publicly because they did not protect the place of correction through God's word and voice in the secret place. When you read Hebrews 12, it notes that correction is meant to yield peace and holiness in our lives.

THE RESPONSE

God is coming and separating even those within the body of Christ who appear to be godly but have chosen other idols and gods. We cannot have both. We can only have one, and I love this because the fruit of knowing the One brings liberty to every part of your body, soul, and spirit. You will always be where you need to be, responding in humility, love, and celebrating the kingdom of heaven on earth. The wheat enjoys the abundant life that so few choose.

He is consistently tapping our shoulder to get our attention in the secret place so that we don't have to have our shortcomings broadcast for all to hear. When we don't have ears to hear Him in the secret place, He will send a friend or acquaintance, and when we don't listen to them, it manifests publicly. What's hidden in secret cannot be hidden for very long. We are 100 percent responsible for how we choose to respond to Him. He never reveals the issues of our heart without bringing a solution for us to replace it with.

The tares rage with jealousy, anger, division, malice, slander, judgment toward others, and are really good at making everyone think they are godly. Scripture is very clear that Jesus will send angels to come and collect the tares and weeds and throw them in the fire. This should totally put the fear of the Lord in us to love what He loves and to hate what He hates. This should inspire us to live a life in response to the Holy Spirit. This should also empower us to go into the world and make disciples so that He can gain a massive, righteous field of wheat.

I want to encourage you to invite the Holy Spirit into every dark place and thought. Let Him be your leader in the tiniest to the biggest things. What role do you play in the harvest? How can you help prepare yourself as the bride for Jesus, and how can you help prepare others? We need Him more than ever, and He sent His Holy Spirt to lead us and teach us.

PRAYER

Holy One, thank You for Your leadership and friendship. Please reveal to me any part of my life that is leading me to deception. I desire to be led by You and You alone. Help me love those around me and to stay true to the convictions in my heart from You. I want to be filled with You and part of Your harvest, Lord. Amen.

Chapter 10

Unwavering Faith

By faith we understand that the universe was formed at God's command, so that what is seen was not made out of what was visible.

—HEBREWS 11:3 NIV

What a way to start a chapter. Lean into the line "what is seen was not made out of what was visible" and then just drop the mic and hit the prayer room. We serve a God who made something from nothing. This Holy Revolution will require great faith to believe He will do what He said He will do. As the darkness gets louder in areas of our society, we cannot let that shake us. We must be ready to hear the word of the Lord and do exactly as He calls us to do so that light can invade the darkness with solutions fueled by immense love.

You better believe the enemy will do everything he can to keep us from agreeing with God and what is in His heart. When you have a dream, a promise, or a word for a situation in your heart, it will be tested, you will go through the fire, and it's important to embrace all of these moments in order to grow in faith and come out stronger. Faith shows up when things look impossible. When the world is laughing or shouting one thing, heaven is whispering the answer and looking for those who will agree with God and partner with Him until that promise manifests on earth. It could be a word for our nation or a personal word in your life or a friend's life. Regardless, there is nothing like the jaw-dropping moments of faith in action.

What do we do when everyone around us doesn't see or believe what we do? What do we do when we feel hopeless and don't feel like we can stand anymore? What if we didn't really hear God and we are on the wrong path? There are so many questions that come up when we are standing in faith, and I have learned that these are healthy. They help us to evaluate where we really are and understand what we really are believing in. It's important for us to dive into God to discover the true answers when they arise. Do not let peoples' lack of faith or negative past experiences keep you from agreeing with God.

HEARING GOD FOR YOU

Faith, then, is birthed in a heart that responds to God's anointed utterance of the Anointed One (Romans 10:17 TPT).

We have heard many times that faith comes from hearing the word of God. When we hear testimonies of what Jesus has done in our lives, when we read about Him in scripture and we are truly listening with the ears of our heart, something is birthed in us to believe that He will do that again and again and again. There is a substance of faith that comes into our hearts and causes us to stand in agreement with Jesus to do everything He said He will do. It is a tangible knowing deep within you and a conviction that fills you. Faith is a knowing that you can't escape. It is important for us to hear this for ourselves and be intentional here.

I always find it very important to remind people that yes, you do hear the Lord. He is speaking to you. The question is, are we seeking Him for the proper interpretation or are we assuming we know what it means and only hearing what we want? If we hear the Lord and are filled with the wisdom of the earth, we are interpreting with a worldly lens. When we seek Him to really understand what the meaning is behind it, we find Him and what He is truly saying. He tells us to seek Him, which means sometimes we need to send out a search and rescue team for the interpretation. Just kidding, but seriously, we need to remain humble here and seek Him until we discover the King's revelation.

I have been in situations and so have my friends when it was crucial for us to know directly from the Lord what to do. When my husband and I were dating, we had some influential and wonderful leaders encourage us to get married or move on. What we really needed was healing in our own personal hearts before marriage came along. So both of us leaned into the Lord for leadership and guidance during that time. We were not pridefully ignoring what some of these men and women shared. We took it before the Lord and said, "God, if this is true, will You please show me because I want to walk in Your ways." He also revealed leaders who were praying into our situation and sharing wisdom with us on how to walk in that season. What does this have to do with faith? Sometimes, the promises that have been spoken over us will be tested by amazing people, and it's important to hear from Him what to do so that we can be unwavering to the sound of *Him* inside us.

I had two friends whose marriage went through a massive shaking. I remember sitting with my girlfriend in tears and prayer when the news first broke. I felt the fear of the Lord in the car. She didn't know what to do in that moment but had a deep relationship with the Lord and has always desired His plans for her life. I knew this was a moment when I could not give her my opinion or try to share what I would do. I could pray with her and love her, but this was a moment when she needed to know from the Lord what she was going to do so that when the testing and trials came she wouldn't be upset for listening to friends, but she could be reminded of what the Lord invited her into. She chose to stay and their marriage is getting stronger and stronger, and this has been a difficult but beautiful adventure for both of them. Getting a word from the Lord in an absolutely crazy situation is very important. Their lives are fully dependent on Jesus and have been transformed because of faith. When everything looked hopeless and lost and broken, they grabbed on to the word of God in faith and have fought beautifully with the Lord for their relationship.

So I would apply this to any promise you believe God has shared. Do not just rely on the words of the prophets. Seek Him and ask Him for the interpretation of what was shared. Submit it to someone who will pray with you and seek the Lord for understanding, and then actively stand in this place with Him the way He is leading you to. When you learn to personalize faith and not just do what others would tell you to do in a situation, you become unwavering in these places and spaces. He wants to share His plans and dreams with you. Will we take the time to listen and agree with Him?

THE SHAKINGS

Now faith is the assurance of things hoped for, the conviction of things not seen (Hebrews 11:1 ESV).

What happens when people don't see it, people don't agree, it doesn't look like it will happen, you get slandered, someone projects their doubt onto you, your expectations are not being met, or it's not happening the way you want it to? This is where we really get tested and it can be very healthy. Whatever needs to be shaken here will be, and it will reveal to us what our faith and hope really are in. Are they in the outcome or are they in the Lord? Is it in what people say or is it in the Lord?

> *Trust in the Lord with all your heart and lean not on your own understanding; in all your ways submit to him, and he will make your paths straight* (Proverbs 3:5-6 NIV).

It's important to embrace Jesus where everything looks impossible. It's important to remind ourselves that we do not know what will happen apart from the Lord revealing it to us. Faith is believing what God has said even when we cannot see it. When we know and trust God's voice, we will become unshakable men and women in the kingdom of heaven who stand regardless of what's going on around them. The path ahead will be clearer as we keep acknowledging that He is Lord of the situation.

Do not be discouraged when things look like they're not going to pan out the way He said. This is where faith comes into action—when you can't see it yet. We have followed and we have seen so many men and women in the word who stood against all odds.

Imagine being Noah. He's building this giant ark, and in that day this ark was no small thing. Okay, that thing wouldn't be small today, either. Everybody's like, "Have you lost your mind?" But because he knew the Lord's voice, he continued in obedience to build when people laughed. Imagine—all anyone needed to do when they saw Noah build the ark was turn their own heart to the Lord to see if this was, in fact, what He was saying. But because of human wisdom they couldn't comprehend what God was doing.

> *But God chose the foolish things of the world to shame the wise; God chose the weak things of the world to shame the strong* (1 Corinthians 1:27 NIV).

God uses the foolish things to confound the wise. It is not human wisdom that allows us to see what God is doing, but it is by His Spirit that God's secret wisdom is revealed. So it will require unshakable faith for us to build with God what He's called us to build, and we get to partner with heaven in order to see these things come to fruition. So, like Noah, people may call you crazy, but when the rain starts pouring down and the flood starts coming in, they will know that you heard the Lord.

My heart is for everyone to know what God is saying. I don't want anyone to miss the adventure of being on the ark with us in all that God is going to do on the earth. Think about each of us who are called to help eradicate abortion, overturn evil curricula in schools and replace them with true, identity-driven curricula, lead revivals, fight for equality with the message of heaven, expose the evil fruit of pornography and make it unthinkable as well as helping end sex trafficking in your nation. Each of these things will require hundreds and thousands of people fighting in unique ways and at different levels. However, we have seen many times that there will be people who don't see or understand and aren't afraid to let us know.

God is always saying "victory." When we are truly turned to Him, His desires become our desires, and He always has a win. I have learned to appreciate seasons of shaking because they test everything you need to know and establish even more of what you do know. Promises are really valuable, but the journey leading up to them is just as valuable.

> *And without faith it is impossible to please him, for whoever would draw near to God must believe that he exists and that he rewards those who seek him* (Hebrews 11:6 ESV).

It is a promise in His word that He rewards those who seek Him. God delights in us believing in Him in the impossible circumstances. Imagine all of heaven watching us and cheering us on when it looks like hell has won, yet here we are believing and knowing God is still going to blow that victory trumpet and we are celebrating before we see it!

PROMISE VS. PROMISE KEEPER

I remember going through seasons (yes, plural) when I allowed the promises and dreams in my heart to be clinched in my fists so tight that the journey to the promises became miserable and, dare I say, my idols. Sometimes I was like a giant toddler throwing a temper tantrum in the middle of the prayer room because I did not understand God's ways or timing. It looked impossible so I was mad, hurt, confused, and an emotional train wreck. I was staring at my watch thinking it should have already happened and been a smooth journey, so what's wrong, God? The Lord was so kind and gracious to me, but there came a time when the true test of the journey was me believing so much that He would do what He said He was going to do that I was willing to lay it all down for Him to bring back up in perfect timing. I was able to enjoy life and give my all to whatever I was doing.

This doesn't make sense to the world because the world would tell you to fight for your dreams and promises in your own strength. There are promises that come along that are better fought for in prayer and belief in your heart than with your own hands. There are other promises that require hard work and preparation to get to. If we begin to worship the promises and gaze at them too long, we will lose our minds to them, and ain't nobody got time for that. Are we just wanting the promises, or is He really going to be enough for us? Selah.

I have learned that He is my ultimate promise. Living a life set apart with Him is where I find true satisfaction, and being led by the Holy Spirit fills my life with the fruit of the Spirit to walk in love, joy, peace, long suffering, kindness, goodness, faithfulness, gentleness, and self-control.

As a visionary it is a gift to be able to dream of, believe in, and declare the wonderful things that are coming, but we can also, on the extreme side of this, make idols of those dreams. They should never consume us. They should be a fun thing to dream of, steward well, and pray for with God but not in a way that keeps us from being present in the moment. Our dreams can submit to the substance of faith within us, knowing they'll come and knowing we can still enjoy the adventure with God. He is our great reward. He is the one we will be spending all of eternity with.

THE WHISPER IN THE CROWD

My husband, Lance, and I have a very unique dating story. I feel as though our journey to the altar of marriage was preparation for me to understand how I hear God and understand that in every promise the promise keeper is greater than the promise. In the beginning I held on to the promise of marrying Lance tighter than I did the Lord. I quickly learned it was important for me to lay him down, even if it was me laying him down before the Lord over and over again, until I really understood what that meant.

This promise came with testing. It came with us going on a break and me sitting in my closet sobbing and crying out to the Lord. I remember one or two times even using curse words to express the level of pain I was feeling as I spoke to God. When I heard myself in those moments, I discovered how immature I really was in that season of my life. Side note—I never felt God be angry at me when I was speaking like this in my closet. I felt His delight in my honesty, and I would quickly repent for what was coming out of my mouth from my heart. That junk came out, and I invited Him into all of those ugly spaces.

When I would sit and weep in my closet, I would thank God for what He had done in my life. As I thanked Him, I was coming into agreement with and gratefulness for all He had done in the past. Reminding myself of how faithful He has always been with specific memories brought me into His presence. Then I would declare what He said as I poured my guts out to Him. I would begin to laugh and repent for speaking to the Lord like that because I was overcome with how faithful He is, how faithful He has been, and how faithful He always will be.

From the time I knew Lance was my husband to the time I walked down the aisle to him was five and a half years. With one four-month break and one seven-month breakup during that time frame, many people on the outside had formulated their opinion and were not afraid to share it with us. I learned quickly that the words of man would cause me to shift and question the Lord at times. It was very important for me to lean into the Lord and what He was saying and have the Holy Spirit direct me to men and women who were praying for us and who could also hear the wisdom of heaven in our situation. I wanted what God had for me and I wanted what God had for Lance more than the opinions of people.

My weapons of warfare during this season were fasting, praying, listening, and learning how to interpret what the Lord was saying. I was also surrounded by friends who would fast and pray for the situation I was in. They told me what I needed to hear, not what I wanted to hear. I knew I heard the Lord. However, I would literally pull away from the crowds and the opinions of others to hear the Holy Spirit and Jesus on what it meant until I knew where to partner my faith. These things helped anchor me in who God is so that when people gave their opinion I would know in my heart what God said in those moments without shifting or changing, because He never does.

Once we were engaged, I realized that it was never about me marrying Lance, and it became more about whether or not I heard the Lord. Hearing God is everything and pulling away from the hustle and bustle of the city is important to lean into God. As we have talked about in previous chapters, even Jesus pulled away from the crowds. This is vital to our walk with God and to remaining in faith. The crowd will always be shouting, but the whisper of heaven is what we need to hold on to in the season of believing and agreeing with God.

Sometimes we can really be off or the promise can be an idol. Walk close in community with people and mentors who will help you grow here while you're standing. It can be hard to hear correction, but it helps us stay in the right direction. If you don't have those people yet, ask Holy Spirit to bring them into your life.

MIRACLES OF FAITH

One of my close friends was battling infertility for a few years. She and her husband had experienced eight losses in pregnancy. She had several direct words from the Lord, I had a few dreams about them, and several others had prophetic words or dreams about them carrying full term. There were many of us who were standing in faith with this family. We got so into standing and agreeing that she would call me and tell me she was pregnant and we would freak out and celebrate together before it actually happened. I know this may sound crazy to some, but we fasted and prayed for God's words to prevail even though we couldn't see it yet. The joy of the Lord became our strength during this time of prayer.

When you seek the Lord on your journey of faith, He gives you specific things to stand on. In this case there were so many, but one was about twins. She would take notecards of words and lay them out in front of her in prayer time and declare them. Fast forward—they chose to go the adoption route. They met with the birth mom on February 14 and the baby girl came on February 19, much faster than they thought. Eleven days after they had their baby girl of hope, they found out they were carrying in their womb. They had conceived the day they met with the birth mom. This means they have Irish twins. God just brought them creatively to their family. There is so much more to this story, but I want to encourage you to be faithful with the words He shares with you. There were moments when pain came in because of the losses. We cried and wept together and allowed ourselves to grieve, but then we continued to stand in the word of our Lord.

ACTIVATING OUR FAITH

I highly encourage you to activate your faith with God as the Holy Spirit leads you. My friend who walked through many losses in pregnancy purchased a baby bag as a statement of hope and faith, knowing she would have a baby one day. She now owns a baby bag company called Hope Bag to encourage other moms to have hope in their journey.

When I was single and desiring to be married, I started a prayer journal every day for a year to give to my husband when we got married. My husband, Lance, wasn't even in the picture at this time. This gave me an entire year of seeking God, learning to hear His voice more, and listening to what He had for me rather than what I had in my mind for me for a husband. I also collected items for my future spouse in a treasure chest to give to him one day when we got married. God told me my husband was a rapper and that is rare. He also showed me a picture of my husband praying for someone and they got out of a wheelchair and walked. There is so much more God revealed to me, and all of them are in my husband Lance! This was me activating my faith in a promise with creativity, knowing that it was building faith as I listened to what God was saying.

Celebrating is one of my favorite things to do when I can't yet see a promise fulfilled. Whether it's celebrating for debt being completely paid off, celebrating a family member's salvation you're believing for, or that new job promotion, there is something wonderful about putting your heart in a position of thanksgiving. It's also a great way to remember that God is faithful to do it and all you need to do is believe!

Decrees are a really big way to stand in faith with God. Where has this promise you're waiting for been fulfilled in the word? Read it and declare it over your own life. What prophetic words have been spoken over your life? Decree it out loud and write it down. Keep decreeing and believing. Remember, the Lord commanded things into existence that had no substance before. He created them with His words, and we can do the same. We have a lot of authority in Him, and it's time that we see heavenly things invade earth.

If you don't want to stand alone in your journey, invite a prayer warrior friend in with you whom you trust. Someone who prays and seeks the Lord for what He is saying and can come into agreement with you. At the beginning of my journey with Lance, I would call my friend Jirat in California and Ashley in Texas. We would celebrate and pray and believe together for what God was saying. None of us moved from that place of knowing God is faithful, and it helped us all grow as we stood together for something special. It was awesome to have them stand with us the day Lance and I got married. I also want to share with you that there is something special about us partnering with other people's dreams and promises. Other people's victories with God become our victories when we partner with them until we see God do what He said He was going to do.

Creativity is another great way to connect with faith. I know a woman who battled infertility and wrote a song about her future child. She sang this song and believed for pregnancy and carried full term! Another friend had an unhealthy thyroid and kept sketching and drawing a healthy one and believing hers would be healed. How amazing is this? Now she is whole and well. What about visualizing yourself in the place that requires faith? Can you see yourself there? Do you need to create a dream board about it so you can see it each day in your room? What about commissioning an artist to do a prophetic painting for you over something? I love creating prophetic art pieces for others to stand and agree with God in. These are powerful ways to grow in faith and connect with faith.

PRAYER

Lord, You are the victory when everything looks impossible. Teach me Your ways, Lord. I desire to hear Your voice and understand Your ways. I desire to be one You find faith in and one who stands no matter what comes our way. I love You, God, and I thank You for being You. Amen.

Chapter 11

BATTLE PREPARATION

God never intended the journey to a promise fulfilled to be miserable.

The battle is often won because of the hard work and discipline that was put in between point A and point B. The victory of the revolution is won because of the character that was forged in the fire, the hours spent learning from mistakes, the moments of choosing God when your flesh was screaming another option, and oh, so much more. In this Holy Revolution, many of us will find that because we were faithful to keep fighting the great fight of faith with God and not give up, the battle will be won.

OIL IN OUR LAMP

When opportunity presents itself, it's too late to prepare.

—JOHN MAXWELL

This is one of those quotes that has impacted my life. My friends Audrye and James shared this quote with me after they attended a John Maxwell event. It's not scripture, but it does line up with biblical principles and certainly struck a chord within me. It reminds me of the parable of the ten virgins. Many of us have heard this parable, and I encourage you to go read Matthew 25 and meditate on it if you haven't heard of it. Every one of us is on a journey right now with the Holy Spirit. He is preparing us as a bride for the bridegroom, and when He comes it will be too late to prepare. In this parable five of the virgins had prepared oil in their lamps and extra for the journey, and the other five were not prepared and ran out.

Five were trying to live off of other people's oil and did not realize they needed their own. Let that sink in. How many times do we live off of other people's oil? Whether it's listening to a sermon, attending a well-known church, an encounter someone had with God—I could keep going. These things are not bad, they are great, but our personal intimacy, history, and love with Jesus is far weightier. Are we having our own true storehouse built with God when no one is looking? Are we paying the cost of preparation to maintain oil in our lamp for every journey ahead?

We are all storing oil up right now whether we realize it or not. Everything we take in is part of our baggage and storage for the coming days. It's often in times of shaking or course direction from the Lord that we discover what type of "oil" we have stored up. Is it doubt? Is it rebellion? Is it hope? Is it faith? Is it toilet paper? (I had to.) God has one oil for us. It's an oil within that can only come from the filling of His great love, and it is unshakable. It is also very personal for each of us. No one else can pay the cost for our oil. Only we can collect this oil with God.

Therefore, the journey is necessary to help us learn, grow, and become the very bride He is longing to return for. The journey teaches us how to keep oil in our lamp. If you signed up for a body-building competition, you wouldn't go on stage if you had not prepared for the event. When you sign up to be part of this Holy Revolution, you are signing up to embrace the journey of preparation and discipline to face each opportunity ahead. This is the same with following the Lord. At all times, we are to be ready for Him and preparing our hearts for every "yes" along the way.

Opportunities are coming our way whether we are prepared or not. There are going to be opportunities for promotion, and how well we are stewarding this current season will be reflected in the future season. There will be persecution and accusation coming your way. So, is the word of God and the love of Christ stored up in you so that you can pour out the blessings instead of reacting with something other than Him? People are hurt, lost, and broken, and they will stumble into your path. Are you praying for God to prepare you for these moments so that you can know how to encourage the person in front of you? There will be moments when the sick will need healing—have we stored up the word in us to know that God will actually do what He said He will do so that our brothers and sisters can recover? Revival is coming to the church and outside of the church—are we storing up scripture and adoration for Jesus so that when it comes we are able to help bring in the harvest of souls so hungry to know Him? So many opportunities are coming, and what we store up now will shape our reaction to these moments in the future.

PLOT TWISTS

The American dream is painted as a life of freedom and success that anyone can strive for with continued opportunity for growth. This is often seen as men and women working hard to reach their deep desires, build their own income, build their own structure of success, and have comfort with luxury. You have a dream inside your heart. The only way for you to see it happen is for you to work tirelessly to make sure it comes to pass, no matter the cost. This spirit is hovering and weaving itself all throughout America and other nations.

I myself have been caught up in this very dream several times. I used to believe that I would make a lot of money and then sow into the kingdom of heaven with that money. That dream is the faux version of what Jesus intends for us to surrender to. I felt the

Lord tugging at my heart to paint full time during a season, and I did not have the confidence in myself to move forward. I had no idea how to truly be a successful artist at the time. I was looking for what I was carrying rather than trusting in God for what He was leading me into.

At that time, I was pursuing a career in which I could climb the corporate ladder. The problem was, I never heard or felt the Lord lead me into that corporate lifestyle, and when I really thought about it, I felt I wasn't to pursue it. I saw it and heard about it and assumed it was the normal, and I wanted the cultural approval of that lifestyle and the money.

I was miserable in the corporate job. I absolutely loved the people I worked with, but the job itself was one in which men and women would call me, screaming over the phone and belittling me. I was scheduling nurses for a company, and it was really hard for me to get up in the morning to go to work because I was miserable in this job. I would drive 45 minutes to an hour each day to work and then I would drive 45 minutes to an hour each day back home. It was an hourly position, and I did not make enough to live on my own.

I was fresh out of graduate school with a master's degree in communication and absolutely miserable, unknowingly filled with pride and entitlement. Little did I know what shaking was coming while "living this dream." One evening I had a literal dream in which two scenarios played out. One thing you have to keep in mind is that the Lord speaks to me very clearly in my dreams. Oftentimes, I will dream something and it will happen, so I knew to pay attention if I had a significant dream of some kind. The first scenario was me getting fired. In the second scenario, I put in my two weeks' notice, and at the end of both scenarios I was painting. I knew from my dream that if I didn't put in my two weeks' notice, I would be fired. I didn't know what I was going to do other than paint, so I turned in my resignation letter within two weeks of having the dream.

Guess what! When I went in to speak to my boss, she told me that she thought she was going to have to let me go. I was so shocked because the dream was going to play out and God, in His kindness, showed me a way He preferred it to play out.

So I began painting full time and spending most of my free time in the prayer room at our church or at home praying and painting. I watched God show me how to put my trust in Him because I had been living a lifestyle in which I could work hard and provide for myself. I remember one day I needed to pay one of my student loan payments and it was the day it was due. I ran into a woman who had commissioned me to do artwork in the parking lot and she wrote me a check for the amount I needed to pay that loan payment that month. It was a miracle for me.

What did I learn from this lesson? While we seek Jesus and pursue Him as our leader and teacher, He hands us His dreams for our lives—assignments and dreams we were created to carry out on earth as it is in heaven. God's plans for our lives cannot be attained through building in our own strength, making plans in our hearts, or doing what we think we should do. I am not encouraging everyone to quit their job and live in the prayer room of their church, but there is something about experiencing firsthand the provision that comes with being led by God on each of our personalized journeys. This is a heart posture and not a picture of your bank account. You could be a millionaire living a surrendered life to Jesus in this way.

> *A man's heart plans his way, But the Lord directs his steps* (Proverbs 16:9 NKJV).

I feel like this was the anthem of my 20s: "Jamie Lyn made plans in her heart, but the Lord kept ordering her steps."

"Lord, Your ways have made my heart come alive more than I could have ever asked for or imagined. I have discovered Your character and Your love even more. I would have never chosen the things You have invited me into, Lord, but I am discovering You more and more through them."

As I continued to surrender to God's plans, it led me to the children's ministry at Upper Room, my church in Dallas. I never in my wildest dreams thought I would be a children's pastor. I didn't think ministry was even a real job because that spirit of pride was marinating in my thought life. It turned out to be one of the most incredibly rewarding things I have ever experienced in my whole life. I learned to be led by the Holy Spirit as I worked with a team to create and build the children's ministry. Serving the children and teaching them to hear the voice of God, pray, and be led by the Holy Spirit produced heavenly character in me. It also helped me grow and mature.

As I served these children, I then moved into the position of the communication director for our church. It became a hunger, joy, and delight to work there. I was painting on the side as an artist and eventually went back to painting art full time. This also surprised me because I really enjoyed working at the church. I struggled even telling people I was a full-time artist because it wasn't the dream that was in my heart. Yet it was preparing me in character for what God had for me down the road, and it was what I was called to steward well and be faithful in. I was on a journey, discovering how to be led by the Holy Spirit rather than being led by my own personal dreams.

Your dreams could be waiting on a family member to be saved, opening a restaurant, living in a new city, starting your own company, preaching, writing a book, having children, traveling more, multiplying your resources, or even tapping into a new level in your spiritual walk. These things are absolutely beautiful and really important to God. We must know that our Husband in heaven isn't there to tease us with these passions and dreams. The things within us are from Him, and He will open doors of opportunity and favor for us as we continue to move forward toward Him. In the meantime, we get to position our heart to delight so much in the Promise Keeper that we enjoy the journey and adventure of getting to the fulfillment of promises with Him.

OUR WAY VS. YAHWEH

You never know what you are learning in a previous season that will help make the next season much easier.

God did not design the journey to each promise to be miserable. I believe He designed it for us to persevere, grow in character, and become a mature bride in Him. When I graduated grad school, I thought I was going to change the world immediately. Little did I know, God wanted to change *my* world so that my heart could be transformed. Doing things God's way instead of our way teaches us to trust Him in every season and in everything, to hear His voice, and to discover who He created us to be all along. How can gold become purified without the refining fire? In order to walk into the promises and dreams in our heart, we must first submit to the leadership of the Holy Spirit.

I always wanted to be a preacher, author, and television show host. The world would tell you to write the book, to start messaging people, to advertise your name, and to go intern at a television show so you can learn and grow. All of that could even sound like wisdom. When I was baptized in the Holy Spirit, it changed everything for me. I was being led by something greater than myself.

Instead of following the wisdom of the world, I decided to follow the voice of God. He took me into a job that I had no training for. I knew nothing about being a children's pastor, but I knew how to go to the Father and learn. Therefore, I learned to build something *with* Him and I learned the humility of serving in a deeper way than I had known before. Serving children taught me how to develop a sermon for all the media messages I do now; it helped me grow in the word of God and taught me how to equip the body of Christ in spiritual gifts. It also taught me about child-like faith. The word of God means what it says. He will do what He said He will do every time. He is exactly who He says He is, and now I pray according to these truths with faith and agreement in all of who God is. Sneaky, sneaky our Holy Spirit is.

Also, graduate school was something I never thought I would do. When I was in children's ministry, I knew how to write a training manual because of the immense number of papers and thesis writing I did. You never know what you are learning in a previous season that will help make the next season much easier. The entire time of following God in my 20s taught me that I will go anywhere God calls me to go and I will do it with trust and patience. I was so impatient in my early 20s, but because of His leadership and me submitting to Him in obedience and love, I learned it is far more enjoyable and there is a purpose, whether I can see that purpose or not, in being led by Him alone.

PREPARATION

When God tells you something, you better buckle up that spiritual seatbelt because there is possibly a journey of preparation ahead, and, Lord willing, we will be faithful during that time to hold on to Him and let Him prune every branch that isn't bearing good fruit along the way. When we do this, we will bear even more fruit in the next season. If God calls me to lead, people will be eating fruit from my life. I want my fruit to be pure, holy, and righteous. I want people to know Him by the fruit in my life. Therefore, preparation is very important—pruning and all.

You are holding in your hand a promise that was spoken to me from the Lord 13 years before it was published. My preparation for this book has been falling, getting back up, looking at Him, getting distracted, then repenting and looking at Him just to find out that looking at Him is really the most satisfying place to be in all the earth. I am so grateful you are not reading whatever I would have thrown together right when He spoke that word to me. I am almost positive nothing in that book would have pointed you to the man Jesus.

Every single thing God invites us into, even when it looks nothing like the dream you have painted in your heart, is for a purpose. He doesn't let any season go to waste, and if we truly keep our hearts turned to Him in every season then we will bear much fruit in those dreams when they do come.

STEWARDSHIP

Whoever can be trusted with very little can also be trusted with much, and whoever is dishonest with very little will also be dishonest with much (Luke 16:10 NIV).

There is a level in which we learn to steward the words, gifts, and promises God has given us on this journey. God has put many gifts and talents within each one of us, and there is a fire and magnifying glass on the creative ones He is raising up in this Holy Revolution. What is it that you want to do full time? What are the prophetic words that have been spoken over your life? It might be that you will be a singer and songwriter. Are you writing songs in your journal with the Lord and singing? Let's say your dream is to pastor a church. Who are you pastoring when no one is looking? You want to lead women? Are you someone women can trust with their secrets and heart issues? Are you faithful to pray for other women before you have a title to go with it? What about stewarding millions of dollars? How are you stewarding hundreds of dollars? Are you being faithful with what God has given you now?

If you want to learn how to play the piano supernaturally, then what are you actively doing to learn? Have you signed up for lessons or purchased a keyboard? You will never know if He answered your prayer until you get in front of the piano and start playing. You don't always go from nothing to all of a sudden playing in Carnegie Hall overnight. It will require your stewardship. The Holy Spirit is a great leader for revealing to us what we can do to prepare in each season and how much time to put to it.

My husband and I love to rap. We used to freestyle a lot more back in the day than we do now. I remember going up during prayer and just freestyling to the Lord. This is a gift you have to keep doing and flexing each day in order to stay solid at it. Because we were practicing when no one was looking, we were able to worship the Lord publicly with this gift during that season. We had the honor of rapping on the first album at our church because we were in a season of stewarding our gifts well. Favor comes upon those who are faithful.

If you want to see healing every single time you pray, that is amazing. Every time Jesus laid hands on the sick, they were made whole. He said we can live like He does, so, yes, that is our inheritance. But how can we expect to see healing if we are not filling our minds with the scriptures about God's love for us and miraculous healing? Also, are we going out and laying hands on the sick and believing and praying until we see it happen every single time?

It's important to steward these dreams well in our hearts. Character is built along the way, and the great teacher leads us and equips us to do it the way He created us to. I love this line and cannot remember who I first heard it from: "Do not ask for in public what you are not doing and contending for in private." This also wakes me up to believe for and contend for the things I desire to see one day.

> His master replied, "Well done, good and faithful servant! You have been faithful with a few things; I will put you in charge of many things. Come and share your master's happiness!" (Matthew 25:21 NIV)

When we learn to be faithful with these treasures that God gave us, He begins to give us more. No matter what season you are in, steward everything He has given you as though the platform for that gift is already massive. Plot twist—heaven is watching you and that platform, even in the secret place, is pretty huge. The way we treat something when no one is looking is pretty indicative of the way we will treat it when people are.

You can only "hide" things for so long. Even the time we steward with the Lord each and every day requires discipline. The size of our platform will be the size of our fall if we are not stewarding our hearts before Him well. Keep your heart watered by the spirit and fed by the word. Continue to be discipled by the man Jesus and serve others well. He wants to be part of your journey and prepare alongside you. The fruit of our lives is the fruit of how well we have stewarded our hearts and gifts when no one was looking.

SERVING

Offer hospitality to one another without grumbling. Each of you should use whatever gift you have received to serve others, as faithful stewards of God's grace in its various forms (1 Peter 4:9-10 NIV).

On my journey with God, I have found myself doing things for an extended period of time that I used to judge or that I never thought I would be doing. The Lord put grace on my life and gave me unique gifts to be able to do these things in service to others in each season. For example, I lived in Mozambique for three months one year for a missions school. I really wanted to cook for the permanent staff members and create a unique and special night for them once a week. Part of that is because I *love* hospitality, and the other part was I am super relational and wanted to pour into them. However, the school really needed artists who could paint signs for each of the new churches they were building across Mozambique. So I ended up painting signs and using my gift to serve, because that was the greatest need. It was such an amazing time of connecting with others who were painting the signs as well. At first I was bummed because they switched my outreach, and then I realized the Lord was inviting me to use the gifts He gave me to serve. Serving isn't always the popular, shiny, flashy thing. It's often the place or space that is overlooked, hence the reason why people need so much more help in that area.

Have you ever met someone, or been that someone, who complained because of all the tasks they had to do? I know I have been around those people, and I have been that person as well. Can we be real and say that person is not fun to be around? I didn't even enjoy being around me when I was complaining. If you are going to choose to do something, do it with joy and without grumbling or don't do it. Paul even mentions in First Corinthians the warnings from Israel's history. He said that those who grumbled were killed by a destroying angel. Y'all, that is very intense, but we have most definitely read and heard about the Israelites in the desert so many times as an example of not complaining. If complaining is coming out of your mouth, it is a good indicator of what is in your heart. We should take these moments seriously and present them to the Holy Spirit to help us cut off at the root whatever the true issue is so that we can serve with all joy.

For even the Son of Man did not come to be served, but to serve, and to give his life as a ransom for many (Mark 10:45 NIV).

Jesus is our great teacher, and as students who follow Him and learn from His ways we quickly learn that our lives are meant to be of service to God and to people. The world shows success as those who are of high esteem, who have great influence and are affluent in all of the earthly treasures. The kingdom of God measures success by the posture of our heart and the fruit of our lives. Our King did not come with a giant crown, in royal robes, or ruling thousands of people the way many thought He would. He came as a servant to millions of people and gave His life so that we could inherit the riches of heaven within each of our hearts. He is still serving us today as the great intercessor for each of us at the right hand of our Father right now.

If you are Gen Z or a millennial, we still have a lot more serving to do before we step into the epic things God has for us down the road. However, if we can learn to see how He is moving throughout the journey, it will be so much more fun than focusing on what we want that's possibly not for another ten years. This is crucial.

I want to encourage each of you reading this to be quick to serve where there is a need. I am not saying that you should say "yes" to everything someone asks you to do. That would keep you from saying "yes" to everything the Lord is calling you to. Are you willing within your heart to volunteer to serve in a capacity that might be outside of your comfort zone? Maybe you want to volunteer in a role that looks cooler, but really the Holy Spirit might be asking you to serve where no one can see you. This is real, y'all. We need to be honest about that flesh that wants to be part of everything that's hype. What about children's ministry where there is usually the biggest need at churches? It's so overlooked, yet God is in that place. What about cleaning the bathrooms? What about picking up the room after the service, not because someone asked you to but because you see it's a need? What about making sure the older people in your community have groceries in tough times or company to visit with? What about asking Holy Spirit who you can bless today and doing it? Maybe you can serve your city or state by running for office. You don't have to be given an opportunity or title to serve formally, to be a good servant. The Holy Spirit is wonderful at showing us how to serve others well, and serving is a posture of our hearts before God and man.

> *But when you give to the needy, do not let your left hand know what your right hand is doing, so that your giving may be in secret* (Matthew 6:3-4).

Also, we don't have to post about the hidden places we are serving. It's okay to just keep these moments between you and God. I really wanted to mention this because I believe this is something society has trained us to do. Jesus was clear in His Sermon on the Mount, and I want to encourage you to invite the Holy Spirit into this place of your heart and conversation. When you give or serve, the world doesn't need to know. I feel like it can rob us of our treasure in heaven. Just enjoy being present and let it be something you do because you get to do it with the Holy Spirit.

Serving is also a characteristic that our platforms should never be "too big" for. When you learn to serve joyfully at the "lowest level," when no one is looking or praising you for it, you will understand the true meaning of being a king or priest. You begin to learn that leading is all about serving others. Serving also gives you room to be in someone else's shoes who does this for a living. It allows you to see how important every role in the body of Christ is.

I have learned a great deal by serving people who are ungrateful and unkind. It's taught me that I am to serve without expectation of a thank you or anything else in return. It's taught me how to love people well no matter what position they hold. When you can get to a place that you don't *need* someone to notice you serving them, I feel as though you are in a great place.

> *Whatever you do, work at it with all your heart, as working for the Lord, not for human masters, since you know that you will receive an inheritance from the Lord*

as a reward. It is the Lord Christ you are serving (Colossians 3:23-24 NIV).

People will not always see serving the same way you do, and it's important for us to remain kind and not have expectations of others to show up like we do. After all, this isn't about other people serving the way we think they should. This is us coming before the Lord and serving Him by serving others. I have felt the presence of the Lord when scrubbing toilets. I have felt the joy as I vacuumed an empty building after someone's wedding or after service. There is something joyful about serving people and finding Jesus while you're doing it. Always be willing to serve people when they need help.

ME, MYSELF, AND I

Do nothing out of selfish ambition or vain conceit. Rather, in humility value others above yourselves, not looking to your own interests but each of you to the interests of the others (Philippians 2:3-4 NIV).

I have met people and also been this person myself who was so immersed in me, myself, and I that I couldn't think of others. I was praying for myself, fighting for myself, thinking about myself, talking more than listening—this list could go on. The moment I looked away from me and began to serve and pray for others, I felt a weight lift off of my life and discovered that I was made to pray for others when they are not around. I was made to pray for hurting people with love and encouragement. I was made to find out how I could help those who need help. When we stop living for us and we begin looking outside of ourselves, a whole other dimension of our nature in Christ is revealed. We discover what we were made to do all along—serve.

I have found immense joy in serving people even when I wasn't where I hoped I would be in life or in the position I desired. Serving others helps us discover the heart of Jesus even more and keeps us from being so self-invested. I would encourage you to ask the Holy Spirit where you can serve in your city, your church, or the community around you. Ask Him if there is a specific family or person you can sow into through prayer—someone who needs help throughout the week.

This is a posture that shouldn't stop even if you became the most powerful person in the world. Leadership is serving. It's not dictating and being the person everyone looks to because you are powerful now. Anytime we are promoted by heaven, it is because we have served others well and stewarded what He has given us well. So if you are promoted in some lovely way in your job, community, or dreams, do not forget to keep the heart posture as one who serves.

It's wonderful to always be ready to "clean the toilets" and encourage those who are. Reach out to the people you are leading and ask them how you can be here for them in this season. Ask them how you can pray for them or give them prophetic words. We can do nothing on our own when we choose to follow Him. Our will becomes the will of the One who sent us, and in that we find ourselves serving the hell out of this world, literally.

THE WAR OF PERSECUTION

It is inevitable, as we move forward in our journey of building with God in this Holy Revolution, that persecution is going to come. Anytime you stand for something this pure and radiant, there will be people who do not understand, and they will tell you in unique ways. Persecution allows us to experience the truth that Jesus is our everything. When you begin to experience the hate and the accusations that come to those who are walking with Christ in this season, it will forge character that can only be forged through experiencing what Jesus also experienced. This character will be forged when we choose to respond and live the way Christ did as our holy example. We are walking into days that are darker than before in the natural. However, we get to see even more of the glory of Christ as we grow in maturity to persevere and be who He has called us to be.

> *They said to you, "In the last times there will be scoffers who will follow their own ungodly desires." These are the people*

*who divide you, who follow mere natural
instincts and do not have the Spirit* (Jude
18-19 NIV).

There are Christians and unbelievers without the
Spirit who will begin to bring even more division in
the church, and we will get to experience extend-
ing mercy to them before judgment. I used to be a
Christian without the Spirit, and it has taught me to
be able to love and come from a place of understanding why someone would lash out at me. I myself used
to assume a lot about others and tell them off before
ever asking them for understanding because there is
a possibility I am wrong. The shocking part of this is
that most of the time when I would react to someone
rather than ask them what they meant by something, I
was wrong and I wasn't hearing their heart.

Jesus did not fight with weapons of earth; He
walked in humility and love and allowed God to defend
Him when most of us would fight to defend and justify
ourselves when we are misunderstood.

Learning to be hidden in Christ as He is our
great defender will be one of the most beautiful ways
to experience His love. His kindness is what has
led each of us to repentance time and time again.
Therefore, I have recognized in times of persecution from others that I can come in low and remain
kind because anything other than that will put fuel to
the type of fire I am not meant to burn in. I encourage you to read the tiny and extremely short book of

Jude. It is a powerful revelatory book on walking with mercy and love toward those who do not yet have the Holy Spirit.

I have never been more misunderstood and had posts taken out of context than I have in the year 2021. Every single person who has accused me has never reached out to hear or understand. It grieves my heart because I am so relational and I love people so much, but it's also taught me to live the life Jesus preached about in His word. I don't see the levels of earthly accusations and persecution letting up moving forward; I definitely see an increase. With that, there is also an increase of experiencing the glory and love of Christ.

There is a political spirit that is always right and only wants to win merging with a religious spirit that is filled with law, and neither have mercy within. It will be important for us to remember that we are not against flesh and blood. Our brothers and sisters are not the ones we are at war with. We have all been extended mercy when we didn't deserve it; therefore, how much more should we extend it to others when we have been wronged?

Please, be quick to forgive and ask the Holy Spirit to fill you with love for the people who do you wrong. This is such a powerful tool as we prepare for every battle. Patricia King calls it the "love war" when we are persecuted or come across someone who triggers something in us. We must discover love in these places. Keep your heart pure before

Him and allow Him to correct you if you respond with hate. Also, be quick to apologize when you are wrong and repent before the Lord. Humility, prayer, and loving our neighbors are the true weapons of this war.

PRAYER

Holy Spirit, I thank You for Your friendship. Thank You for filling me with Your wisdom on this journey with You. Help me see where I can serve, what I can steward well, and how I can prepare to do all that God has called me to do. I love You and I want to know You on this journey. I desire to discover more of who You are. Thank You for leading me. Amen.

Chapter 12

GOD'S SECRET WISDOM

I am a solution-driven woman, and I have learned as I continue to mature and grow in the Lord that when I see something I don't like it doesn't mean that it is time to complain. No, it means God has a solution for it, and it's time to ask Him what the solution is. Complaining about issues in our nation or in our world is a really easy thing to do. Anyone can do it. Complaining about it in our head is not any different from complaining about it with our words. So when we see a problem, we can train ourselves to ask, "Father, how can I help be part of the solution or what would You like me to do with these feelings of frustration?" Sometimes it's prayer and other times it's a plan of action to impact earth with heaven from the place of prayer.

Christians are to be implementing the innovative and creative ideas on the front lines that people are responding and reacting to because of the Spirit of God and creativity within each of us. However, we have found ourselves playing catch-up in many areas because we pulled out and away from what we were called to be the light in because we thought it was too dark. Now the darkness in many of these areas is pretty loud and highly worshiped across the world.

There is much exposure we have seen and will continue to see with abortion, sex-trafficking, education, sexual identity, church leaders, government officials, leaders in businesses, entertainment, media, and more that will continue in the coming days. The question is, what will our response be when it does? This is and should be an eye-opener for the church in how we are called to take down the idols and high places and replace them with the power and creativity of God. You have been perfectly created and designed with gifts, personality, and talents that were made to be part of God's divine plan and purpose on the earth right now. He does not bring exposure to places without having an answer in His hands.

The earth is a superb and excellent place of well-thought-out and intricate beauty. The very thing that was with God as He formed every living thing is here for us to have full access to as we create and build with God. His spirit of wisdom is ready to pour solutions into you and me. Are you ready to be part of God's perfect plans on earth? Warning—no one said it will be easy, and it is not for the complacent. This is for the remnant who know who they are in Christ, who their

God is, and are willing to do what it takes to establish heaven on earth. Best part is, we get to do it with God and invite people into the journey with us! This is the Holy Revolution in action.

THE FEAR OF THE LORD

I am grateful for the fear of the Lord. This is a gift that we get to experience when we have awe, wonder, and reverence of our God. I have experienced a tangible, trembling presence of the fear of the Lord, and I knew, no matter how big or small that moment would seem to anyone else, that I must respond as a holy one who is set apart. I had to do what God was calling me to do in that moment rather than what my flesh wanted to do or I felt like I could die. I know this is an intense way of describing it, but His presence comes in and invades every part of you, and obedience would trump any temptation or desire in this very moment because God is with us. Those who walk in the fear of the Lord are those who walk in the ways of God.

I was speaking to one of my spiritual moms on the phone; her name is Veda, and she is a true intercessor and gift to all who know her. She said that experience brings you revelation that only experience can bring. I believe the fear of the Lord is one of those. I believe it is a healthy and dangerous prayer to ask God to invite you into His holy fear so that you can love what He loves and hate what He hates. It's easy to say what the word says, but the fear of the Lord empowers us to walk in His ways and experience Him in this way.

> *To fear the Lord is to hate evil; I hate pride and arrogance, evil behavior and perverse speech* (Proverbs 8:13 NIV).

Pride and arrogance are what caused satan to fall from heaven for eternity and lose every battle he will ever try to face against the righteous. We must live knowing that God is Truth and at any moment we could actually be wrong and desire His Truth to lead us. Many who walk in pride and arrogance don't know that they are deceived and "deception fills the hearts of those who plot harm" as noted in Proverbs 12:20 (TPT). I am consistently asking the Holy Spirit to lead me into truth and, if there is any area where I am in deception, to reveal it to me so that I can repent and walk in truth. This is a powerful prayer to pray before I ever ask Him to do it in another person's life.

Humility is a marker of the Holy Revolution. Humility helps us walk in the fear of the Lord. If we do not have humility then we cannot respect or recognize God's correction, direction, and protection. Remaining teachable for the rest of our lives before our heavenly Father and those around us, no matter how old or young the person is, is a beautiful and protective posture. We must consider others more than ourselves and remain in our hearts as servants to them as Jesus serves us.

> *The fear of the Lord is the beginning of*
> *wisdom; all who follow his precepts have*
> *good understanding. To him belongs eter-*
> *nal praise* (Psalm 111:10 NIV).

The Holy Spirit helps reveal an adoration for Him to be able to receive and walk in wisdom. The abundance of fruit that comes from the spirit of wisdom is supernatural. I do pray that we would all have a respect and discipline to read the word of God where wisdom is spoken of so beautifully and powerfully. Writing this chapter feels silly when I just dream of each of us picking up the word and discovering more about this gift there. The books of Psalms, Proverbs, James, and First Corinthians are a great place to start. I highly encourage you to read these books and to meditate on these words day and night.

> *The friendship of the Lord is for those who*
> *fear him, and he makes known to them his*
> *covenant* (Psalm 25:14 ESV).

Friendship with God is something that comes to those who walk in His ways. In John 15, Jesus even stated to the disciples that we are no longer servants to the master because the master does not reveal his business to the servants. Jesus came and shared only what He saw the Father do and spoke only what He heard the Father saying to reveal the friendship we are invited to with God. Abraham was even called a friend of God because he believed all that God said to him.

We cannot accomplish this way of living apart from the fear of the Lord.

WISDOM

The fear of the Lord is the beginning of wisdom, and once we are walking in His ways we are able to walk in one of the most beautiful gifts God has given us full access to. Her name is wisdom, and she is pretty epic.

> *But the wisdom that comes from heaven is first of all pure; then peace-loving, considerate, submissive, full of mercy and good fruit, impartial and sincere* (James 3:17 NIV).

The fruit of wisdom is pure, and the pure in heart shall see God. It's filled with peace and love. It submits to the Lordship of Jesus, and it's full of mercy. Mercy triumphs over judgment and is one of the most beautiful gifts we can receive and also extend to others. Wisdom is filled with good fruit. When people eat from wisdom, they will not get sick. They will be nourished. Finally, it's impartial and sincere.

We cannot allow the political spirit to divide us, even within the church. It's constantly screaming, "I am right and you are wrong." Wisdom allows us to see from the heart of God. God isn't taking a political side or the side of your favorite team and bashing the other. He has the view from a different perspective and His wisdom, through His Holy Spirit, allows us to see from this place with Him. It's like the world is fighting over whether the glass is half empty or half full, and wisdom is saying, "Look at the One who is pouring the water."

If any of you lacks wisdom, you should ask God, who gives generously to all without finding fault, and it will be given to you (James 1:5 NIV).

Many places in the word we read about the power of wisdom. This is one of those gifts that is promised to be poured out to those who seek her and those who ask for her. There is not a designated dosage amount God gives us. It says that He gives generously to those who ask. Have you ever been in a situation in which you responded in a way that felt supernatural and "must have been God"? Maybe you spoke and you were like, "Man, that was good and there is no way that was me" in your head? I always assume that credit can go to God's secret wisdom. I am intentional about asking for wisdom because I truly desire to walk in her ways and be her great friend.

As I read through the scriptures regarding wisdom, I like to read about her as though she is a person. When you do, it's like, "Can I please be your best friend?" I desire to walk with her throughout the day, process with her internally, and respond to others with her great counsel. Since I have prayed for more wisdom, I have been filled with more wisdom. Doors have opened for me that only God could open. Wise and profound thoughts come out of me that I could not have known had they not been revealed by her. I am even more empowered to see what God is doing, to hear what God is saying, and then to comprehend it because His wisdom is different from the world's and will require understanding. This is me boasting in the Lord and His gift of wisdom to us.

YOUR SPECIFIC BLUEPRINTS

So many men and women are searching for their great call on this earth. We desire to please God and we desire to do what He created us to do, but what is that? Maybe you're in a situation where you do not know what to do and really need an answer. Asking for wisdom is a great prayer, and by listening for her throughout the day I have experienced wisdom crashing in hard at the most unique times and random moments.

> *You will find true success when you find me, for I have insight into wise plans that are designed just for you. I hold in my hands living-understanding, courage, and strength* (Proverbs 8:14 TPT).

This is one of my favorite scriptures on wisdom in *The Passion Translation.* In other translations they are called blueprints. When we find wisdom, we will find true success, and there are wise plans for our situations that are designed just for us within her. Wise plans that are uniquely made for you that were not made for me or your neighbor. These are specifically designed for *you.*

Not only that, she provides the understanding we need and the courage and strength to accomplish these plans. How many times do we have the answer but we just lack the courage? Wisdom holds courage and strength in her hands for you. So what are you needing to do today? Be filled with the courage and strength to accomplish it and go for it!

PUTTING PEOPLE ON THE CROSS

When I read First Corinthians 2 and really rest in what it says, it causes me to be filled with the fear of the Lord. This chapter talks about the secret wisdom of God that can only be found by God's Holy Spirit. When I meditate on it, it puts a hunger within me to understand the kingdom of heaven more than I could ever understand the world. This following scripture has caused me to cry out for and walk in more humility and wisdom:

> *None of the rulers of this age understood it, for if they had, they would not have crucified the Lord of glory* (1 Corinthians 2:8 NIV).

Human wisdom, which is taught by man, is what put Jesus on the cross. They genuinely believed they were right and were filled with so much pride and arrogance that they couldn't recognize the man they had been longing for. Jesus didn't come with a royal robe, a golden crown, and a mansion like they thought He would. He came as a humble servant to reveal to the most overlooked, poor, broken, hurt, sinful, and more so that they could have a place in heaven for all of eternity with Him and our Father. All they had to do was follow Him. Following Him leads to a life of abundance that so few find.

There is even a place in Matthew 28 that makes me weep each time I read it because this could be any one of us. The guards who witnessed the resurrection of Jesus and saw the angel of the Lord, who came at that moment, ran to the high priests to deliver to them what they had seen. The part that grieves me is that the high priests met with the elders to devise a plan. They then paid the guards to lie and tell the governor that the disciples came and stole Jesus' body in the night. They were so arrogant, prideful, and filled with the wisdom of this world that they refused to allow this miracle from the purest man to walk planet earth to be shared. They were blind and could not see. This lie still circulates in the world today. Why does this make me weep? We could be any one of these religious leaders if we are not teachable and have allowed pride and arrogance to seep in. This pride and arrogance is a fruit of earthly wisdom.

Can you imagine being in that meeting and knowing you needed to speak up, because, "What if this resurrection is true and He really is the Messiah who has been prophesied?" Yet their own personal gain and recognition was threatened by an innocent and loving person. They had no fear of God in them. I share this because God is doing and will continue to do the wildest things on earth. He will also do it through the saints, and if we are not careful we can judge our brothers and sisters and throw them on a cross with our words because we do not have eyes to see, ears to hear, and a mind to understand what God is doing. This requires us to seek the Lord so that we can celebrate our heavenly Father and what He is choosing to do throughout the earth.

> *However, as it is written: "What no eye has seen, what no ear has heard, and what no human mind has conceived"— the things God has prepared for those who love him—these are the things God has revealed to us by his Spirit. The Spirit searches all things, even the deep things of God* (1 Corinthians 2:9-10 NIV).

How can we know if we are walking in the wisdom of God? It's something we are to search out in deep love and expectancy through prayer, through fasting, through worship, through listening, and through the reading of His word. I would like to submit to you to always check your heart before the Holy Spirit. It's important to be really honest with Him because He can read your heart and see all that is happening, so why hide? Have you been praying for the thing or person you are frustrated with? Truly, have you prayed yet? If not, why are you speaking? Have you taken the time to listen to God and ask Him if He is moving through someone, even if that person isn't perfect? Is it Him? He will use imperfect people all the time. Why else would we be reading about the life of Abraham, David, or Paul?

> *The person without the Spirit does not accept the things that come from the Spirit of God but considers them foolishness, and cannot understand them because they are discerned only through the Spirit* (1 Corinthians 2:14 NIV).

I see too often how Christians throw shade at one another or how the news portrays certain events going on in our world with gossip, slander, and hate. When we have human wisdom, it's easy to take this all as truth and regurgitate it. It will cause many to grow deceptive in their hearts, and in Proverbs it talks about how deception plots evil. Do not be the person or allow a person to complain to you about someone who is honoring the Lord on this earth. Jealousy will cause people to not see what God is doing through the saints, and we need to remind one another that the wisdom of God will always come uniquely through the saints and look foolish to the world. Those filled with the spirit of God will find the secret wisdom that will reveal what God is actually doing, what God is saying, and give you the ability to understand it. Those with the Spirit will find wisdom.

I remember in the encounter I had with God from the first chapter in this book, the people who had human wisdom deeply judged and criticized the men and women who were weeping and crying out to the Lord. They could throw their hands up and they could look godly, but away from that building the words flowing from their mouths and the fruit from their lives contradicted the word of God in many ways. Many of them were living in doubt that God really does what He says He will do, which is why they build so much of their lives on their own and then slap His name on it for credit. I don't want to get to heaven and tell God how I built everything I have ever done for Him and have Him respond with, "But you didn't build it with Me, and you didn't know Me while you were there." We cannot lead our own lives. We will fail every time. We desperately need the leadership of the Holy Spirit and the discipleship of Jesus.

BENEFITS OF WISDOM

If I were to mention to you all of the benefits that come with the spirit of wisdom, you would throw this book down and start crying out for her. So I am going to share with you *some* of the benefits that are listed in the word of God. If you are experiencing anything that contradicts these, I encourage you to cry out for wisdom and do not stop until your life is a reflection of these benefits. We can put a demand on His word because it will never return void. There are even more written within the word of God, but here are a few.

- Success and protection (Proverbs 2:7)
- Understand true justice (Proverbs 2:9)
- Save you from wicked words of man (Proverbs 2:12)
- Save you from an adulterous spirit (Proverbs 2:16)
- Keep the ways of righteousness (Proverbs 2:20)
- Prolong your life many years with peace and prosperity (Proverbs 3:2)
- Favor with God and man (Proverbs 3:4)
- Health to your body and nourishment to your bones (Proverbs 3:8)
- Blueprints for any situation you are in (Proverbs 8:14)
- Empowers kings to reign and rulers to make just laws (Proverbs 8:15)
- Generous one will govern the earth (Proverbs 8:16)
- Unending wealth and glory (Proverbs 8:18)
- Fill your life with treasures (Proverbs 8:21)

- A word for every day (Proverbs 8:34)
- Fountain of life pouring into you (Proverbs 8:35)
- Every year more fruitful than the one before (Proverbs 9:11)

WISDOM CALLING

Wisdom is crying out on the streets and in every place of influence for those who are listening for her. It is never too late for anyone to turn their heart to God and receive the spirit of wisdom. Wisdom pours into the lives of those who hate every form of evil. She is speaking to those who are listening. Ask the Holy Spirit to reveal any bit of pride or arrogance that could have seeped into your heart. Ask Him to show you if there is anything within you that could keep you from having the full measure of wisdom. Once He reveals this to you, repent from that evil thinking and invite the spirit of wisdom to come fill every place.

It is okay to pray for exposure to come into areas where deception has crept in. I never pray these prayers without first asking Him to expose anything inside my heart that is not Him. It's okay to be frustrated when you see something in your nation, family, a friendship, your job, your church, or more that you don't like. What is most important is that you ask God how you can pray into the situation and if you are to be part of the solution. Wisdom will give you wise plans for any situation you are in. We really need her to accomplish all God has for us ahead in every sphere of influence. All you need to do is ask. Praying in these situations keeps us dependent on Jesus and keeps us from trying to figure everything out on our own. We are not God and we never have to be, thank You, Jesus! We are not meant to do this alone. We are meant to do it all with the Holy One.

Oftentimes, the things we feel burdened most by are the things we are called to help serve. I love what my father-in-love, Lance Wallnau, says, "When your passions and your gifting meet, you will find your calling." So what are you passionate about? What makes your blood boil a little bit? What are the things that people compliment you in all the time, and do any of those passions or gifts overlap? This could be a great indicator of your call. Can you imagine getting to do something that you aren't only passionate about but that you are also good at? God is definitely launching our generation into new places and spaces. We are part of this Holy Revolution. Just some food for thought.

My prayer is that we would all walk in the ways of God and that we would be filled with the wisdom of God. We are never in lack when we walk in holiness, and we are always protected by heaven on this narrow path. Darkness cannot dwell in the light. Therefore, let us shine brighter than we could have ever thought or imagined in music, business, creativity, medicine, our families, teaching, our spiritual gifts, and more because the spirit of all of the solutions, the spirit of wisdom, is leading us.

PRAYER

Holy Spirit, thank You for giving me eyes to see, ears to hear, and a mind to understand what You are doing. I ask for You to reveal to me any area of my life where I am operating or agreeing with human wisdom. Forgive me and fill me with the wisdom of heaven so that I can walk creatively with You in favor, courage, solutions, and strength. I want to be part of Your plans on earth as it is in heaven. Amen.

Chapter 13

TO THE VERY END OF THE AGE

Plot twist—Jesus always wins!

WE ARE THE AVENGERS

I know everyone has different feelings about Marvel movies, but I am going to give an example from *The Avengers: Infinity War* and *Endgame* movies. This example gives away the ending. It's a spoiler alert. I don't like it when people share what happens in a movie before I see it, but they have been out for a while, so hopefully we are good. Also, Jesus gives away the end before we go through it all, so I'm just being led by example. Wow, I feel winded from that long preface.

I love watching superhero movies. They make me feel so strong and powerful as a woman of God. Oftentimes, the Lord speaks to me through movies, and this is one I had to share because what He revealed to me through it is so indicative of the Holy

Revolution. So, let's hop in here as I summarize the movie very briefly to share the prophetic picture of the Holy Revolution.

The Avengers are superheroes who fight off the bad guys, duh. This huge bad guy comes along named Thanos. Thanos is the most powerful evil guy they have ever faced. He is in search of all of these stones that are hidden within each superhero world, and once he collects all of these stones he will have the power to take out half the universe by literally snapping his finger. None of the Avengers are strong enough to take him on alone or even several together. They are trying to beat him to all of these stones.

Thanos is the leader of a massive army of darkness. I'm going to call the bad guys demons. The Avengers can kill these demons on their own and then there are some that require a few of the Avengers to take on. Thanos is like a giant principality. At the end of the first movie, Thanos collects all the stones and takes out half the universe. No one ever thought the Avengers would be defeated, but it looks as though Thanos won. Half the Avengers were taken out with this ending, and it's mind-blowing.

Part two opens up with one of the most overlooked Avengers, Ant Man, who just warped back from a time travel to see the destruction that happened while he was gone. He had the brilliant idea to undo what Thanos did. Long story short, the Avengers worked hard to come up with a plan to bring everyone back who was lost.

At the very end, Thanos finds out the plans and is fighting the Avengers. It's a moment when it looks like Thanos might win again. There is only one way for the Avengers to win out of millions of options too. Thanos and his entire army are facing the Avengers. All of a sudden, all of the Marvel characters and their armies begin to appear to help fight Thanos and his demons. They just kept showing up in droves to support taking out this dark principality. It gave me chills. It literally took all of them in unity to take him and his demonic army out. There is so much more to that movie, but follow me here.

We are stepping into times that will require us to work together in unity to take out principalities in our cities, states, and nations and then replace them with heavenly dwellings! There will only be one way to win, and that's with Jesus at the helm. It may look like the enemy has already won in various situations, but the remnant knows the sound of their Father's voice will be the final word. We will move forward with a triumphant victory. He always wins.

Let's just say that those stones can represent territories or spheres of influence on earth, like entertainment, business, education, etc. It will require humility, wisdom, strategy, love, and courage to influence these places and spaces. We will have to learn to serve alongside people with other gifts, personalities, ethnicities, and age groups. We will need to grow in such love for one another that we are not afraid to die for them in order to accomplish our goal of destroying the works of the enemy and empowering others to know Jesus as Lord of their lives. The vision of the Lord will keep us focused and united.

> *When there is no clear prophetic vision, people quickly wander astray. But when you follow the revelation of the word, heaven's bliss fills your soul* (Proverbs 29:18 TPT).

Jesus chose twelve disciples who were unique and diverse, and they all had their love and reverence for God in common. The Avengers didn't all agree with one another and were unique and powerful in their own way, yet all of them had to learn to work together around the same clear vision and word. This will be a powerful time of us uniting around the word of the Lord and showing up to serve the vision as best as we can. We need one another, and I love that God even sent His disciples in sets of two so that we wouldn't be alone on our journeys. You may be surprised, too, where He sends you and where you end up serving. It will be made clear to you by the leadership of the Holy Spirit. I get so excited thinking about the tough yet successful adventures ahead for all of us with Him and one another.

In First Corinthians 12:14-20 it discusses all of the different parts of the body and how well they work together when they know who they are. We will get to discover the power of respecting the call on other people's lives who are not the same as our own and being there for them when we are called to be in order to accomplish all God has for us. We take care of our foot or our shoulder when it is hurting. We also utilize these body parts when we need to accomplish what we need to accomplish each day. This will be the same in the Holy Revolution of set-apart men and women. We will take care of those who need to be taken care of, and we will celebrate the parts of the body of Christ who will be needed in each hour. This revelation will be beautiful and radiant as we move forward together.

We have been battling demons, but it's time for this generation to take on the principalities with God and His mighty army of warriors. We need one another. We cannot do this on our own. Remember, there will be times when it looks like the enemy has won, but the resurrection life is lurking within the remnant to raise what we thought was lost, up from the dead. This Holy Revolution will know that Jesus always wins. Are you prepared to give everything up to train? Are you prepared to lean in and be led by the Holy Spirit? Are you ready to be filled with love and serve the hell out of this world, literally?! We need you in this remnant. Everyone is called and few choose. The choice is completely up to you.

ANSWERING THE GREAT COMMISSION

The more informed you are, the more courage you can walk in.

We can see all over the news a reflection of how well the church has done at discipling our nations. You can look at the climate of different spheres of influence and see how well we have done at taking care of the sheep and preparing them for the shakings of this world.

I love reading the word of God. It is filled with stories of men and women who have gone before us to help us see the importance of our hearts being completely turned to God. Look at the disciples. We can all see ourselves in them. The fishermen, tax collector, thief, a politician (zealot), and tentmaker. None of these are trades you would think of today. Today, many would imagine someone going into the church and finding the twelve most holy and devoted Levites to be discipled by Him. However, Jesus went into the world and made disciples of those who were in different trades.

Then Jesus came to them and said, "All authority in heaven and on earth has been given to me. Therefore go and make disciples of all nations, baptizing them in the name of the Father and of the Son and of the Holy Spirit, and teaching them to obey everything I have commanded you. And

*surely I am with you always, to the very
end of the age"* (Matthew 28:18-20 NIV).

Fam, this is called the great commission because
it is one of the ultimate places of instruction from our
Lord Jesus. When we chose to become a Christian, we
chose to come into agreement with His word as our
baseline. Therefore, it is time to start making disciples
in our communities and making sure they are water
baptized, baptized in the Holy Spirit, and filled with
the word of God that He has taught us to obey. What
He has done for us, we get to invite others into. It's
that simple. Other people's eternal lives depend on
it. Literally. Where are we called to go into the world
to make disciples? How can we do this without being
tainted by the world? In Matthew, Jesus said:

> *You are the light of the world. A town
> built on a hill cannot be hidden. Neither
> do people light a lamp and put it under
> a bowl. Instead they put it on its stand,
> and it gives light to everyone in the house*
> (Matthew 5:14-15 NIV).

We were not called to be the light of the church.
Uh, oh! We are called the light of the world that cannot
be hidden. What gifts has the Lord given you that you
are called to steward and glow and grow in? Music?
Art? Entertainment? Fashion? Finance? Innovations?
We must not be afraid to run into the world shining
our bright light for all to see. We need to have courage

to push past our greatest fears and into the places and spaces we were made to shine in. However, if we are not discipled well, we will compromise, lose our witness, and fall. Heavy words, but we must be prepared and equipped to do this marvelous work. It's never an easy journey, but it can be flipping awesome when you are doing it all with Jesus at your side.

OBEDIENCE

Obedience is a necessary trait for all of us where we are headed. Obedience kicks in when we don't "feel like it." When you want to snap at someone because you woke up on the wrong side of the bed but instead you choose love. When that judgmental thought comes in and you spike it out of your mind with truth even though you felt like agreeing with it. When you feel like someone you're pastoring just "does not get it," but instead you choose to keep praying for them and asking God for wisdom to lead and serve them. When temptation comes to partner with the lusts of the flesh and we turn to God rather than the flesh because we know it's the right thing to do.

The great commission tells us to teach people to obey all that Jesus has taught us. He was tempted and chose obedience over and over again. It is more than possible to do the same. We can obey Him all day long, but if we don't have love it means nothing. Loving Him is the key, and with love comes a desire to obey.

When I was first doing prophetic art, I was painting live during worship sets. Mind you, I took four years of art in high school, but I didn't do anything in college because I didn't think I could paint full time. It can be really intimidating doing a speed painting of prophetic art in front of an audience. I remember being embarrassed at times because I felt like it looked like a five-year-old painted it. Each time this would happen, someone would come up to me crying, not knowing I was mortified by how elementary the painting was, to tell me how they connected with the Father in that painting. I remember being relieved that it touched someone, and it began watering seeds in my heart for another moment to come.

I was telling my mom and crying about how embarrassed I was to be an artist and how elementary I felt like my paintings were. I was ready to throw in the towel on part of my call. I am not overexaggerating when I say I was done with art on this night forever. Then my friend Bob called me. He was leading inner-healing sessions at our church at the time and began to tell me that he was in a session with a young woman who could not connect with God. She had never been able to see Him. He walked out of the room and grabbed a Jesus painting I had done to show her. He said that in that moment she began to weep and connect with the heart of our Father and was forever changed. I wept like crazy because something broke off of me. It was like, "Jamie, this isn't about you and what you think about it; it's about you knowing that if I have called you, then I will show up and touch people with your 'yes.'"

This is one of my token moments with God that reminds me that even if I don't think or feel like I have enough, my "yes" to God is really important and can change people's lives. Every time I was embarrassed by a painting in the past, I remembered it had allowed someone to connect with God on a deeper level. I continued to show up to blank canvases, confident that whatever He wanted me to create with Him in that moment would be more than enough. I was being obedient beyond my feelings to learn a beautiful lesson with Him. What do you need to show up in obedience to today?

He also asked us to obey His commandments and to teach others and help them obey His commandments. When we fall madly in love with our Savior, we can't help but trust Him to be faithful for it. Obedience is saying, "This moment isn't about me or what I want; it's about knowing this is what He would do in this moment." Are we willing to give away the money we have been saving if He leads us to? Give away that car? That house? Give up that show? Remember those "What Would Jesus Do?" bands we all wore when we were younger. The action part of that is obedience. It looks really good on our wrist, but it's costly to walk in His ways and incredibly rewarding.

FUTURE HOUSE OF PRAYER

For my house will be called a house of prayer for all nations (Isaiah 56:7 NIV).

In scripture, Jesus calls His house a house of prayer. This is the place where we will gather and we will be transformed by the very presence of our Jesus. Then I believe the Lord will fill the saints from this place of prayer with wisdom, revelation, and vision to go into each sphere of influence to make disciples and be the light of the world.

I see the church being the biggest provider of food for those who are going without, not the government. I see the curriculum in education changing and becoming more holy because of the incredible ideas God is giving men and women in the church that will impact the education system. I see the church being able to step in and give stimulus checks for the cities rather than us relying on our government because we operate in such an abundant mindset. I see the church coming alongside businesses and businesses coming alongside the church to figure out how to reach the entire city faster. God has big plans for us, but it will require us not all working within the four walls of the church. We will have more impact in this harvest by taking the light we have found inside the man Jesus and going out into the world.

Churches each carry a different mandate and will start coming together more as a family to help serve their cities. Where one is the arm, the other may be the leg, and another may be the heart. There is unity coming in the churches. There are amazing churches that are transforming cities; Trinity Church in Cedar Hill, Texas, and Open Door Church in Burleson, Texas, are absolutely phenomenal at serving their communities. Their cities are their church, not just the people who show up on Sundays. This is a powerful switch of lens we will need, and we can pray it through together. Upper Room Dallas is a praying church that teaches men and women to be walking, living, and breathing houses of prayer. This will also transform spheres of influence. We cannot expect our leaders to be the ones doing it and taking us into the city; we must we must go ourselves. What is the Holy Spirit leading you to do?

What you create and how you shine is a reflection of the way you have leaned in to be discipled. This army will be filled with men and women who are influenced by Jesus only. Our leader created everything beautiful, you see. He has wise inventions for us to take part in. This revolution will know the voice of God so clearly that their songs are written from a place that brings unity, love, and answers to social injustices. It will be filled with fashion that is innovative and new that doesn't compromise on holiness. It will be filled with brilliant ideas to protect our earth and the land. It will be filled with men and women who are truly being led by wisdom's blueprints that were designed just for them. New media networks will come from the righteous ones. New television shows. New movies. New leaders in government. New books and creative curriculum. It's going to be a wild adventure!

To accomplish the very creative and innovative dreams in God's heart, we must know the leader and helper, Holy Spirit, whom Jesus sent us so that we can make sure we are doing all that we are called to do in excellence. We must know the word of God so that when the enemy comes to twist it in our sphere of influence, because he will, we do not give in to the compromise. Doors will open quickly and the failures we experience along the way will not tear us down. They will be seen as moments that help us grow. Then, we can lead others through these spaces and places without having to experience the failures we have. This is discipleship—to follow Jesus in all of His ways and to teach others to do the same.

GENERATIONS WINNING TOGETHER

It will be important for us to be covered by local churches and pastors who can speak into our lives and point out the areas that could be our pitfalls if we are not careful. I love having spiritual mothers and fathers in my life. I love submitting new things I feel called to build to the Holy Spirit and to my mentors and leaders who bear great fruit. When we walk in humility and appreciation for this kind of leadership and love, we will grow so quickly and have a safety of accountability.

*Honor your father and your mother, so
that you may live long in the land the Lord
your God is giving you* (Exodus 20:12
NIV).

I also want to encourage you to listen to men and
women who are decades older than you. I believe this
scripture is also about spiritual parents around us.
Serve their ministries or businesses. Learn from them
and allow them to disciple you. Respect and honor
their voices in your life. We must never think that we
know more than they or that we should be where they
are today.

They have paved a way and gone through decades
of difficult journeys with God to get where they are
so that you can be where you are today. The younger
generation should never try to overtake the older generations. We should serve them well and always make
room for them. Honor them and allow the Lord to pro-
mote us in His perfect time. Then we can take what
we have learned from them and disciple others with
it. This isn't just an age thing; this is a heart posture.

Think about all of the incredible young men and
women who are coming after us. We get to prepare a
way for them to know Jesus, and because of our courage to tear down idols and high places and seek the
Lord, they will go even further. Our goal in this revolution is not just to achieve victory in our lives but to lead
others through and help them learn how to lead others

one day to victory. This is true discipleship. It's our greatest commission. Warriors discipling warriors.

> *So Jesus said to them, "Truly, truly, I say to you, the Son can do nothing of his own accord, but only what he sees the Father doing. For whatever the Father does, that the Son does likewise"* (John 5:19 ESV).

Remember, we are not alone and we have the great leadership of the Holy Spirit to fill us and lead us everywhere we go. I love that Jesus came to show us how to live. The scriptures about Him and from Him will help us grow and become faithful disciples in a world that is corrupt and evil. His light will shine bright through those who live holy as He is holy and who do what they see the Father doing. We can no longer live according to our flesh but according to the ways of God. You will become a tree of life to all of those who come near you when you live this way.

THE NARROW PATH

We are the Holy Revolution being raised up in this hour. We carry the solutions from heaven that will invade every part of earth. We cannot afford to leave a sphere of influence because we think our voices are not strong enough, unless He tells you to leave it. If He led you there, then He will shine light on all of your ways to accomplish His great victory through you. I guarantee you, you're doing much better than you think you are. Jesus would not have come and shown us how to live this attainable life if that level of freedom was not possible for us. He has called you and me to be holy as He is holy. He has called us to be part of this Holy Revolution. It's now in your hands.

Everyone is called, but few choose. We each have an open invitation to join this highway of holiness with Jesus for the rest of our days. This path leads to the abundant life that so few find with Him. Are you willing to accept the invitation of this lifestyle? Are you willing to let go of the dreams you have to discover the dreams God has for you? I can assure you, this path has brought more freedom and rest to my internal being than I could have ever found on my own. Jesus truly is our everything. It's in living a life set apart that we will find true satisfaction.

PRAYER

Father in heaven, holy is Your name. Your kingdom come, Your will be done on earth as it is in heaven. Thank You for supplying all my needs today; forgive me of all the sins I have committed. I forgive all those who have sinned against me or done me wrong. Keep me holy when temptation comes, and protect me from evil. For Yours is the power and glory forever and ever. Amen.

ABOUT JAMIE LYN WALLNAU

Jamie Lyn Wallnau and her husband, Lance, reside in the great state of Texas. Jamie Lyn is passionate about training this bold generation to hear the voice of God and be the solution. She has been calling generations to holiness through her Set Apart podcast, *The Next America* show, her prophetic artwork, speaking engagements, and social media. She is actively hosting and creating different forms of inspirational media on God TV. Visit www.jamielynwallnau.com to subscribe to her email list and stay updated on the latest news.